C# Developer's Headstart

About the Authors

Mark Michaelis lives in Glen Ellyn, Illinois. He currently holds the position of senior software architect for Real World Technology, which specializes in software for the manufacturing industry. He holds a BA in philosophy from the University of Illinois and has a Masters of Computers Science from University of Illinois Institute of Technology. Mark is also a Microsoft Certified Solutions Developer (MCSD) as well as a Microsoft Most Valuable Professional for the Visual Studio Enterprise product group. He is the author of *COM+ Programming from the Ground Up*. Mark can be contacted at: mark_michaelis@dotnetprogramming.com.

Philip Spokas received his Bachelor of Science in Mathematics and Computer Science from Benedictine University in Lisle, IL and is a Microsoft Certified Professional. He has a vast range of development experience, including all versions of Windows since 1.0, OS/2, and UNIX. He is the vice president of software development at Real World Technology.

C# Developer's Headstart

Mark Michaelis
Philip Spokas

Osborne/**McGraw-Hill**

New York   Chicago   San Francisco
Lisbon   London   Madrid   Mexico City   Milan
New Delhi   San Juan   Seoul   Singapore   Sydney   Toronto

Osborne/**McGraw-Hill**
2600 Tenth Street
Berkeley, California 94710
U.S.A.

To arrange bulk purchase discounts for sales promotions, premiums, or fund-raisers, please contact Osborne/**McGraw-Hill** at the above address. For information on translations or book distributors outside the U.S.A., please see the International Contact Information page immediately following the index of this book.

C# Developer's Headstart

234567890 FGR FGR 01987654321

ISBN 0-07-219116-3

Publisher	Brandon A. Nordin
Vice President & Associate Publisher	Scott Rogers
Acquisitions Editor	Ann Sellers
Project Editor	Monika Faltiss
Acquisitions Coordinator	Timothy Madrid
Technical Editor	Bill Burris
Copy Editor	Marcia Baker
Proofreader	Mike McGee
Indexer	David Heiret
Computer Designers	Carrie Abrew, Peter F. Hancik, Jim Kussow
Illustrators	Michael Mueller, Lyssa Sieben-Wald, Beth E. Young, Greg Scott
Series Designers	Roberta Steele
Series Cover Designer	Greg Scott
Cover Illustration	Eliot Bergman

This book was composed with Corel VENTURA™ Publisher.

Contents at a Glance

Chapter 1   **Introduction to C#** **1**

Chapter 2   **C# Language Review** **15**

Chapter 3   **.NET, the Operating Environment for C#** **69**

Chapter 4   **C# Language Comparisons** **109**

Chapter 5   **Working Within the Bounds of C#** **143**

Chapter 6   **Integrating Legacy Code with C#** **167**

Contents

Acknowledgments . . . . *xi*

Introduction . . . . *xiii*

Chapter 1　**Introduction to C#** **1**

The Component-based Model of Software Design 2

The .NET Approach to Component-based Software Development 5

What Is the .NET Framework 6

　　.NET's Common Language Runtime 6

　　.NET's Framework Class Libraries 9

　　.NET Framework Tools and Utilities 10

Why C# 11

What Is C# 13

Chapter 2　**C# Language Review** **15**

A Simple C# Program 16

　　A Few More Comments on Main( ) 17

　　Adding a Class to the Simple C# Program 17

C# Types and Type Management 18

　　Value Types 19

　　Struct Type 20

　　Enumerations 22

　　Reference Types 23

　　Type Comparisons 25

　　Boxing and Unboxing 25

　　Type Conversions 26

　　Arrays 27

Object-oriented Component Development in C#   28

 Object-oriented Features of C#   29

 Class Constructors and Destructors   40

 Methods   42

 Fields   46

 Properties   46

 Operator Overloading   48

 Delegates   50

 Events   53

Namespaces in C#   57

 Declaring Namespaces   58

Exceptions   59

Attributes   61

Indexers   62

Writing Unsafe Code   65

Documenting Code Using XML   66

C# Coding Style   68

Chapter 3 **.NET, the Operating Environment for C#** **69**

Microsoft IL   70

 How the CLR Gets Loaded   72

.NET Building Blocks   76

 Modules   76

 Assemblies   76

 Application Domains   77

Building Modules and Assemblies   78

Robust Version Control   79

Built-in Metadata   84

 Attribute-based Programming   86

 Reflection   88

Cross-language Interoperability   93

Common Language Specification   94

Common Type System   95

Object-oriented   96

Delegation and Events   98

Memory Management Through Garbage Collection 98

    Garbage Collection Step-by-Step 100

    Finalization 102

    Strong and Weak References 105

Thread Synchronization 107

Chapter 4   **C# Language Comparisons** **109**

Comparing C# to C++ 110

Comparing C# to Visual Basic.NET 127

Comparing C# to Java 132

Chapter 5   **Working Within the Bounds of C#** **143**

Deterministic Finalization 144

    Releasing Resources Explicitly 146

    Variable Declaration with the using Keyword 147

    Reference Counting 150

    .NET Finalization 153

Multiple Inheritance 154

    ATLs Multiple Inheritance In-depth 155

    Containment 156

    Interface Implementation 160

Macros 162

    Combining Macros with Interface Inheritance 162

Templates 164

Source Code Security 166

Chapter 6   **Integrating Legacy Code with C#** **167**

Integration Approaches 168

Calling COM Objects from C# 169

    Using the TLBIMP Utility 171

    The Runtime Callable Wrapper 172

    Method Return Values and HRESULTs 173

    COM Object Lifetime and Deterministic Finalization 174

    Inheritance and RCW Objects 174

    COM Connection Points 174

    Threading of the RCW Components 176

The COM Callable Wrapper, Calling .NET Objects from COM 177
    TLBEXP Utility 178
    REGASM 184
    COM Callable Wrapper 185
    Providing .NET Events to COM Clients 187
    Threading of .NET Components 193
    Additional COM Interoperability Attributes 193
    Additional .NET to Type Library Conversions 194
Data Marshalling 196
    Strings and the MarshalAsAttribute 196
    Marshalling Objects 197
Platform Invocation Services, Calling Unmanaged APIs from C# 199
Interoperability Through Managed C++ 201
Migrating Code 210
Summary 211

Index **213**

Acknowledgments

No book can be published by the author alone, and there are many people who participated in making the publication of this one possible.

In addition to reading each chapter and checking for technical accuracy, Bill Burris, the technical editor, helped with testing the code to make sure that it was correct. Marcia Baker provided copy edit assistance, which is a role we admire, as it is something we not only don't have expertise in, we even lack the patience to try. Timothy Madrid and Monika Faltiss masterfully coordinated routing the manuscript to the appropriate places during tech edits and then through production. Thanks especially to Monika for her extra time during the page proof stages as the corrections were excessive. We also very much appreciate the effort that Ann Sellers put in to making this possible. Her task was especially difficult as she was coordinating a vast number of other publications that would not normally be her responsibility. Her willingness, yet again, to be on the receiving end of Mark's "unique comments and perspectives" was considerably gracious.

Real World Technology, the company we work for, has been extremely gracious in allowing us the time to write this book. Undoubtedly, neither of us would have been able to do this exclusively outside of the office. This was all the more appreciated because the timing coincided with the release of another version of the company product.

Lastly, we are greatly indebted to our wives Elisabeth and Cathy. Writing a book, even one that is only six chapters long, takes a lot of time, and we are well aware that the rest of the world doesn't just stop while the required work is getting done. Elisabeth and Cathy gave of themselves well above and beyond anything that we could have expected. They were incredibly patient and supportive while we toiled away in the early mornings, late evenings, and weekends and even through a family vacation. We are truly blessed by two spouses who are so willing to give of themselves. We'd also like to thank the kids who gave up time with Dad so he could work on "the book".

Introduction

Although C# was announced to the public less than a year ago, there are already several C# books available and undoubtedly more will continue to appear. With this in mind, *C# Developer's Headstart* was designed to be different. Rather than writing another book that focused almost exclusively on explaining syntax, this book covers the syntax in 60 pages and then moves on to some of the more complex and relevant issues relating to C#. By leveraging their existing knowledge of programming, readers will be able to begin real-world C# programming after reading this book.

What Programming Skills You Must Have

Since this book includes a complete overview of the C# language, it is not expected that readers will have any prior knowledge of this new language before they begin reading. However, the book is targeted at enabling developers to jump ahead into programming with C#, rather than becoming bogged down in nitty-gritty syntax. With this in mind, it is expected that the readers of this book will already be programmers with experience in at least one other language. Given this experience, readers of this book will find that they can quickly grasp the essential characteristics of C# within one chapter and then begin examining some of the more difficult areas of the language.

What Software You Will Need

To try all the examples in this book you will need to have installed the .NET Framework SDK Beta 2 or later. This is installed automatically with the Visual Studio.NET, but it can also be downloaded from Microsoft's Web site and installed separately. The authors recommend that Windows 2000 or later be installed, but the .NET Framework is supported on both the Windows 9*x*/ME and Windows NT operating systems as well.

Don't Forget: Code on the Web

Remember, the source code for all of the programs in this book is available free-of-charge on the Web at **http://www.osborne.com**. Downloading this code prevents you from having to type in the examples.

CHAPTER

1

Introduction to C#

IN THIS CHAPTER:

The Component-based Model of Software Design

The .NET Approach to Component-based
Software Development

What Is the .NET Framework

Why C#

What Is C#

C# (pronounced *C Sharp*) is a brand new language developed by Microsoft for its new .NET Framework. The .NET Framework is Microsoft's next development platform beyond Windows DNA for building component-based software solutions. The .NET Framework reflects a huge effort on the part of Microsoft and will most certainly impact most programming done for the Microsoft platform in the coming years. As a developer or a manager of developers, you need to know this technology and you need to know it sooner rather than later. This book's aim is to give you a head start on the C# language, as well as the key features of the .NET Framework on which C# runs.

We expect that when you finish reading this book, you'll have a basic understanding of what C# is and you'll understand how C# fits into the .NET Framework. As no language or platform can do everything, we also want to give you a heads-up on some of the current shortcomings of the C# language, so you're prepared ahead of time for them.

One last note before we start. We want to make every effort to be clear and concise in our definitions, so you know exactly what we're talking about. Marketing departments at software companies around the world (and especially at Microsoft) have already started muddying up the term ".NET" to mean everything from operating system functions, back-end server platforms ("the .NET Server family"), and Web-based service offerings, such as Microsoft's Hailstorm initiative, to any new feature that has been put into a software product for the last five years. The use of .NET in this book, however, should be crystal clear. When we use the term *.NET* or *.NET Framework,* we refer specifically to the bits provided by Microsoft on the .NET Framework SDK. When a feature or function is exclusive to Visual Studio.NET (or VS.NET), then it will be explicitly mentioned.

The Component-based Model of Software Design

Before examining .NET specifically, it is helpful to consider some of the fundamental reasons for which .NET was created. .NET is the current iteration of a technology that has essentially gone through three significant phases. The first significant phase occurred in the early 1990s with the development by Microsoft of a technology called Object Linking and Embedding (OLE) used in OLE Automation. This technology grew out of the need to interoperate the various Microsoft Office applications of the time. Microsoft realized products like Microsoft Word and Microsoft Excel were great individually, but sometimes users wanted to have Word documents that included spreadsheets within them. Rather than duplicating all the code from Microsoft Excel into Microsoft Word, Microsoft developed OLE, which enabled documents from one program—Microsoft Excel, for example—to be embedded into documents of a different type, such as Microsoft Word. On the surface, users could insert a document from one application into another. Under the covers, however, Microsoft had developed a key technology to enable one application to talk to another application. Interapplication communication wasn't limited to the embedding of one document into another, however. Through OLE Automation, one application could call in to a different application, so the first application could manipulate objects located in the second program.

NOTE

One of the key purposes of the first .NET predecessor was to enable interprocess communication with relative ease. Specifically, OLE provided a standard means for embedding a document of one type into a document of a different type and enabling one application to manipulate objects located in a different application.

The next significant phase in .NET evolution occurred with the introduction of COM. As the functionality of a program increased, it became too large and complex to be manageable. Program complexity tends to increase exponentially rather than linearly with respect to the amount of code within an executable. Developers using the *monolithic* approach (one large executable) must have intimate knowledge of both their own code and a significant portion of the other code within the module. In the monolithic approach, a small change in one part of the code could have large and significant side effects in other locations of the program. Not only did this increase development, but it also stretched the testing required to produce quality software.

The solution to monolithic software was the component-based model. In the component-based model, software programs are broken into components and each component offers a different service or set of functionality. Software built in this fashion is sometimes referred to as *componentware*. For example, rather than writing one large executable that includes code for compressing files, sending e-mail, and graphing various trends, developers realized breaking the program down into separate modules was better: one for sending e-mail, one for graphing, and one for compressing files. The separate modules are then combined and presented to the user as one application, even though internally the application may be broken into many different parts, either logically or physically.

When using the component-based approach, each module is independent. Thus, each programmer must manage the complexity of only the component on which he or she is working. Because each component is independent, the internals of one have little or no effect on the internals of another. Through the divide-and-conquer techniques of the component model, the complexity of the application is reduced. Each component can even be tested independently of the systems into which it will eventually be deployed.

 NOTE

The component model reduces the overall complexity of software and significantly reduces the ease of distributing development across multiple companies. Software companies can develop components in the areas where they have expertise, while other companies combine components from multiple companies into a fully functional software package.

Another significant advantage of the component-based model is that not all functionality needs to be implemented by the component developer. If a developer were to create a program for tracking expenses within a company, then this programmer wouldn't also have to write the e-mail program via which expense reports were to be submitted. Instead, the developer would obtain an e-mail component written by another company and simply call into that component to access such functionality. The same is probably true of the spreadsheet control used to display the expenses to a user. Perhaps even the reporting module could come from a third party. The component-based model enables distributed development across multiple companies or departments. In this manner, each company can write functionality in the area in which they're experts and use third party components from other companies when necessary.

Microsoft's implementation of the component model was called the Component Object Model (COM). COM essentially took OLE automation to the next level by extrapolating the idea of interprocess communication to be intermodule communication. Not only would applications be able to interact, but binary modules, such as DLLs, could also be loaded into a process and objects within the DLLs could be accessed. The objects within these DLLs are called *COM components* and the modules in which the object code resides are called *COM servers.* (Note, the term "component" is ambiguous within the COM community. Component sometimes refers to the module within which the object resides—the COM Server—and, at other times, the component is the object itself, whether or not the object is instantiated. Within this book, the component refers to the object itself.).

The component-based model didn't begin with COM. Prior to COM, developers would use library modules that also provided a service. The problem with the library-module approach was that it was both laborious and error prone, both to loading libraries and to calling library functions. Libraries often couldn't be found, and if a version mismatch occurred, the results were usually rather ugly. In addition, the library module lacked a standard methodology. No standard convention for memory management or even a standard calling convention existed. Furthermore, the library model was ill-suited to object-oriented programming and more appropriate to procedural programming. The distinction is this: object-oriented programming extends a basic data structure by defining functions that manipulate the structure and are also owned by the structure. The library model usually just passes data structures and calls functions, rather than passing objects and calling functions on those objects.

After the first release of COM came a technology called ActiveX. *ActiveX* controls were components designed specifically to be hosted within other windows or forms known as *COM containers.* Although not revolutionary, ActiveX significantly reduced the amount of work necessary for creating COM controls by enabling developers to implement only the interfaces that were relevant to their component. ActiveX wasn't a new generation in the .NET heritage but, rather, an improvement to the COM generation.

.NET appeared into this setting. Despite the tremendous offerings COM provided to the component model of software development, it was still lacking in some significant areas.

The .NET Approach to Component-based Software Development

As we begin the third generation of the component model, we also start a new level of interoperability. COM was developed to provide a standard binary communication mechanism between modules. With .NET, the standard moves up from the binary level into an intermediate language called *Microsoft IL (MSIL)* or simply *IL.*

NOTE

With .NET, the standard for intermodule communication moves up from a binary-calling convention and memory-management standard into an intermediate language to which all .NET languages must compile.

In other words, .NET replaces the calling conventions and memory management standards of COM with an intermediate language into which all other .NET languages will be compiled. The result is this: rather than programmers being concerned with ensuring their code will interoperate with an established binary standard, the various .NET language compilers enforce the interoperability by compiling code into IL that automatically is compatible with other IL modules. Rather than developers ensuring they're appropriately performing memory management via reference counting, the .NET technology takes care of automatically performing memory management through a mechanism known generically as *garbage collection.* (The details of the specific garbage-collection algorithm are discussed in Chapter 3.)

One of the key characteristics of IL code that enables many of the features found in the .NET Framework is that metadata is an inherent characteristic of IL code. *Metadata* is data about data; it describes the characteristics of the data. Every data type definition within IL code includes metadata that accompanies the data type, even after the code has been compiled from its .NET language (C#, VB, Managed C++, and so forth) into IL code.

NOTE

A key portion of IL code is the metadata about the data types within a module.

Metadata isn't limited only to the data types themselves but, in addition, the .NET software modules themselves include metadata. This metadata is used at runtime to determine the location of code, and then to load that code, so it can be executed.

What Is the .NET Framework

Now that you know where .NET came from, we'll spend a bit more time defining what it is. This section provides a brief definition that helps put .NET in context. The .NET Framework and SDK itself can be thought of as three distinct technologies: a Common Language Runtime (CLR), a Framework Class Library, and Tools and Utilities.

Each of these is briefly described here so you know what they are, but a detailed description of the entire .NET Framework is beyond the scope of this book. Certain key areas are discussed in various chapters; for example, deterministic destruction is covered in detail in Chapter 5. The .NET Framework isn't something easily consumed or digested in a single sitting, but using C# makes gaining the benefits of .NET easy without requiring intimate knowledge of it.

.NET's Common Language Runtime

The CLR is the heart and soul of the .NET Framework, and is responsible for loading and executing C# programs, as well as programs written in any other .NET language. The CLR itself is hosted by Windows executables built for .NET, for ASP.NET in Internet Information Services (as an ISAPI filter), and in Internet Explorer to enable client-side programming. In addition, the CLR defines interfaces that allow it to be hosted by custom applications if one of the existing options isn't appropriate.

The significant architectural improvements in .NET aren't specific to C# but, as a .NET language, C# benefits from them. In fact, C# receives much of its power from the .NET Framework and the CLR. A quick summary of the key features and benefits of the CLR is as follows:

- ▶ Managed execution of MSIL, including type safety and garbage-collected memory management
- ▶ Rich, built-in type system
- ▶ Security
- ▶ Interoperability with non-.NET software
- ▶ Improved deployment
- ▶ Common Language Specification (CLS)

Managed Execution

The significant portions of managed execution were discussed earlier but we should mention the IL is Just-In-Time compiled into native executable code. This generates a performance hit the first time the program is run, but subsequent executions are quick. If desired, an assembly can also be pre-JITed, thereby removing the initial first-time performance hit.

The managed execution environment also defines application domains that provide an execution and security context over and above an assembly.

Type System

The CLR provides a type system common to all .NET languages and class libraries. A variety of types are supported, including a set of integral and floating point data types, as well as a fully featured string type, a date type, and an object type. The object type serves as the root class for all other types in .NET.

The common type system is a critical element of .NET's language interoperability feature because .NET languages are removed from the burden of trying to define types that can interoperate. At the same time, special language-specific types can be constructed easily from the provided .NET base types.

Improved Deployment

Even with recent advances in software installation and configuration, deployment of applications, both rich client and Web-based-applications, remains a cost-intensive issue facing IT departments. For many functions, rich clients aren't going away anytime soon and advances in their deployment remain critical. In addition, as Web servers become more prevalent, deployment and maintenance have become critical for IT departments faced with deploying perhaps dozens of Web or intranet servers. Even Web clients, especially those that include ActiveX downloads, can run into client versioning issues.

.NET includes advances that allow side-by-side running of assemblies and facilitate xcopy style deployment, in which files are simply copied to the destination computer without needing to be registered. .NET includes the version information in the primary key data of an assembly that allows multiple versions of the same assembly to run on the same machine. If an existing application depends on a particular version of an assembly, another application that comes with a new version of the same assembly won't disturb the original application.

.NET also provides the option of deploying assemblies privately or shared in the Global Assembly Cache (GAC).

Robust Security Environment

Another critical issue facing the software industry today is security. Rampant virus outbreaks have done much to waste both time and money. The .NET runtime directly addresses this and related security issues with several key features.

Assemblies can be digitally signed, allowing verification of the author. This prevents unauthorized code from executing, whether the code is executed from the command line or if a currently running program calls it.

Even though you might be trusted, you might obtain and execute code that shouldn't be trusted. Of course, executing this code wouldn't be your fault, but the damage can occur anyway. .NET runtime security provides a security wrapper that can enforce security even when unauthorized code is executed by an authorized user.

In the spirit of providing a robust and secure environment, the .NET runtime doesn't allow pointer-based access unless the pointers are executed in a secure context and the security to execute this "unsafe" code has been specifically granted. This offers another layer of protection against mishaps both intended and unintended.

Common Language Specification

The .NET Common Language Specification (CLS) enables language interoperability on the .NET platform by defining the rules required for interoperability. The .NET platform itself goes a long way toward making this possible, but without some clearly defined rules, classes built in one language won't be easily consumed by another language.

The CLS itself defines the base types that must be supported by each of the .NET languages, as well as conventions that should be followed. Finally, the CLS enables independent third parties to create language compilers for .NET that can share in the same interoperability features of the Microsoft-provided languages.

.NET's Framework Class Libraries

Previous to .NET, direct access to significant portions of the operating system library were exclusively available to C++ developers or were not well integrated. In some cases, the functionality was even duplicated. The .NET Framework combines and unifies significant work under .NET that has been done in different system areas, such as XML, COM+, and data access (ODBC, OLE/DB, and ADO) or in different tools, such as Visual Basic (VB), Visual C++, and Visual J++. The result is a rich set of classes available to any language on the .NET development platform whether or not Microsoft development tools (Visual Studio.NET) are used.

In each functional area addressed by the class libraries, you can see the evolution from the prior platform including WinForms, ASP.NET, Web Forms, and Component Services while, at the same time, the functionality is provided in an extensible and easy to use class library.

WinForms

The .NET's *WinForm* classes represent the merging of the usability of Visual Basic forms, the power and flexibility of C++'s Microsoft Foundation Classes (MFC), and the class library of Microsoft's Windows Foundation Classes for Java into a rich windows class library that breaks the language barrier. Unlike Visual Basic forms, MFC, or the WFC, WinForms are available to any .NET language.

One advanced feature of WinForms is the support of visual inheritance. Consider a base form class that embeds controls placed on the form. Classes that derive from the base class inherit not only the code functions, but also any of the controls placed on the form. This even extends to exposing the forms in a library-type assembly for use by other assemblies.

Because WinForms are based on the .NET Framework, applications built using WinForms are as easily deployed as any other .NET application, which means xcopy and side-by-side deployment models are supported.

ASP.NET and Web Forms

ASP.NET provides an entirely new set of services and a much-improved programming paradigm for Web development and deployment including built-in support for Web

Services and Web Applications. Again, as a .NET class library, the ASP.NET classes are available to any language of the .NET platform.

Contrast this to the previous version of IIS, where getting access to another language typically required using either VBScript or JScript to call a COM-based object. A workable solution to be sure, but inevitably, this could lead to a cut-and-paste development and "spaghetti script" in even the simplest cases.

A key force driving the .NET Framework and ASP.NET is the capability to develop and deploy Web services rapidly. A *Web service* is a set of software accessible via the Web, which provides some sort of service. This is much like a COM component, except it's Web-accessible, and supports an XML payload and SOAP-based method calls. As such, a Web service is readily accessible to service clients with minimum prior knowledge or special client-side infrastructure, such as a type library.

Component Services Library

The .NET Framework class libraries also provide a complete implementation for COM+ services. This includes access to transactions, connection pooling, pooled objects, and queued components.

Using the framework classes, component services classes are easier to develop. A developer simply derives from the ComponentServices base class. Attributes can also be placed directly on classes and methods to configure and control transactions.

ADO.NET

ADO.NET represents the evolution of the data access methods from ODBC to OLE/DB and ADO. Gone is the hybrid nature of OLE/DB for low-level access and ADO for high-level access. And because ADO.NET is delivered as part of the class library, you implement data classes by deriving from ADO.NET, instead of creating brand new wrappers and embedding data access calls in them.

.NET Framework Tools and Utilities

The .NET Framework Software Development Kit (SDK) includes a couple dozen tools and utilities, such as the base compilers for C#, as well as Managed Extensions for C++, Visual Basic.NET, and JScript. The SDK also includes both command lines and visual debuggers, along with all the tools and utilities required for managing and deploying assemblies. Many of these tools are discussed throughout the rest of this book. The following table lists some of the more significant of these tools.

AL	Assembly generation utility.
ILDASM	Disassembles a .NET assembly into IL code and manifest data.
ILASM	Assembles MSIL into a .NET assembly.
TLBIMP	Imports a COM type library.
TLBEXP	Generates a COM-compatible type library file from a .NET assembly.
GACUTIL	Loads and manages assemblies in the Global Assembly Cache (GAC).
REGASM	Registers an assembly so it can be used by COM components.

Why C#

Now that you know what .NET is about, let's begin a more in-depth focus on C#, starting with why C# was invented in the first place. When many programmers first heard of C#, they grumbled something like "Why did Microsoft have to come up with a new language?" and "What's wrong with Java?" A simple answer to these questions isn't available, but you should be able to answer that question by the time you finish reading this book.

Let's start answering it by describing a simple scenario you may be familiar with. That scenario is as follows: "jock" programmer bangs out a COM component in C++ that does some cool business function, and then writes a test application for that component using Visual Basic. Why isn't the same development environment used for the test application? Clearly, the RAD paradigm of Visual Basic has merit. C# and .NET are there to provide that RAD approach to all languages of the .NET platform, while still providing a powerful and extensible object-oriented language.

To emphasize this point further, the following story is taken directly from these authors' own experiences. Real World Technology, the company the authors work for, chose to develop using Visual Basic for the user interface of our applications because VB was easy to use and there existed a large number of VB programmers. We used C++ to build COM-based business components for speed, efficiency, and the capability to build a rich set of classes to support an object-oriented design. This model of programming in VB against COM-based components replaced an existing proprietary script language and proprietary runtime for that script and extended script libraries (DLLs). A whole host of advantages were gained by using VB as the glue to join not only our own components together, but also to integrate third-party components quickly and easily. As a result, the application's business logic is open to any environment that can speak COM. At the same time, efficiencies gained with this development and deployment model let us rapidly expand the number of features and functions our business objects supported without getting bogged down in GUI changes. C++ lost out as glue that tied components together because of the high cost of doing anything simple, which was also significant. VB lost out for developing business components because C++ was better for building a high-performance, rich and consistent business object model. C# and .NET are positioned so this product development could all have been done in the same language, with no loss of openness or minimizing the exposure of business logic the use of COM has afforded.

While you might think that's an interesting story, we're still left with questions such as, "Why not extend an existing language to fill this void?" and "Isn't this what Java is for?" Let's consider the first question by discussing C++ and VB, two languages with popular compilers provided by Microsoft. (Note, while a number of C++ compiler developers exist, only one provider exists for VB.)

C++ has benefited greatly from being a standardized component-oriented language, but this is also its biggest curse. This is because C++ cannot rapidly mature to incorporate new concepts required for interface and component programming, or incorporate a rich runtime. It's worth noting, this is the gap Java has effectively filled for many developers.

In any event, by the time you get done extending C++ to include what's required for .NET and modern component-based programming, you have a completely different and nonstandard language. An in-depth comparison of Visual C++ to C# is provided in Chapter 4 and Managed Extensions to C++ are discussed in Chapter 6. C++ programs are full of the extra "bits" and programming conventions required for component programming. Changing the language to support these features natively isn't an option.

In fact, VB—because it's controlled by Microsoft—has actually gone through that metamorphosis and has caused no shortage of controversy in the VB developer community. Visual Basic.NET is effectively a new language that leaves Visual Basic 6 (the prior version) behind. Even with that, VB has a stigma attached to it as not being a "real programming language." C# is an easy to use language that doesn't have the stigma of VB attached to it. It is expected that C++ programmers won't be embarrassed to admit they know or use C# and it's well known that most C++ programmers apologize for using VB whenever they get a chance.

While this might seem silly at first, if you think about what this means, it helps provide useful insight into what C# is about. Even with many wizard-like modern programming conveniences, component programming in C++ still requires extra work that isn't relevant to the solution at hand. VB (6 and prior) is incredibly more "programmer efficient" for building simple Win32 applications. However, VB becomes increasingly difficult to use as system sizes increase because of its lack of true or deep object-orientation and limiting, though powerful, runtime.

Now we turn to Java. The story here is short, thanks to the outcome of Sun's lawsuit. Microsoft's attempts to turn Java into a development platform for Windows brought them the wrath of Sun's lawyers. The outcome of this lawsuit has effectively ruled out Java as a language choice for .NET. After reviewing everything in .NET, and the different approaches taken, it's tough to see how Java could have been used as the language and not suffered the same fate as Visual Basic and C++ or, in effect, turned into C# in some form anyway. Once the lawsuit concluded, Microsoft was prevented from changing Java significantly enough to fit well within the .NET environment.

Having no other real options, a new language designed specifically for the platform was the only way to go. Whether this is exactly the way things went inside Microsoft is difficult to say (probably even for most Microsoft insiders), but the bottom line is this: with C#, Microsoft (and its inventors, Anders Hejlsberg and Scott Wiltamuth) was able to design a language starting with a clean slate. What they came up with is a clean, simple, and modern design that directly addresses the needs for component-based software development.

What Is C#

With that as a prefix, we can now start to get into the C# language itself by describing what it is.

As a new language, C# can be component-oriented from the ground up. It is built to support key features of .NET natively. C# doesn't need to maintain a legacy of features or syntax. Constructs required to build components are native to the language. This includes features such as properties, events, interfaces, and attributes. At the same time, the language is designed in the C/C++ family, so it's a language familiar to C++ programmers.

C#'s goals are to provide a simple, efficient, productive, and safe component-oriented language familiar to C/C++ programmers. C# is a fully object-oriented language designed to build software components for the .NET Framework. C# is the de facto language of the .NET Framework as indicated by the fact that key pieces of the .NET Framework are actually coded in C#. Microsoft indicated "millions of lines" of C# code were written by the time of the Microsoft Professional Developers Conference in September 2000, at which C# and .NET were first officially introduced to the developer community.

Some of the highlights of C# include:

- ▶ Object-oriented and type safe
- ▶ Type safety
- ▶ All types are objects, and developers can extend the type system simply and easily
- ▶ A rich and complete set of class-based metadata is available, and this metadata can be extended by the developer
- ▶ Key component constructs are native to the language
- ▶ Heap-based memory is automatically garbage collected
- ▶ Direct access to the vast .NET Framework class libraries

C# and the .NET Framework are a natural evolution of programming language and services. For years, programmers have been requesting object inheritance and better type safety in Visual Basic. Programmers have spent many, many hours programming the plumbing of COM interfaces to build component-based systems. C# and .NET are direct answers to these efforts.

C# and .NET continue the evolutionary movement of system-level responsibilities from the realm of the application developer to the realm of the operating environment, so developers can concentrate on what they're paid to do: develop great applications.

CHAPTER 2

C# Language Review

IN THIS CHAPTER:

A Simple C# Program

C# Types and Type Management

Object-oriented Component Development in C#

Namespaces in C#

Exceptions

Attributes

Indexers

Writing Unsafe Code

Documenting Code Using XML

C# Coding Style

In this chapter, we review the key features of the C# language. A detailed language review would be a book in itself, so the details in this chapter are necessarily brief and to the point. However, all of C#'s features are covered, so when you finish reading this chapter, you'll have a complete picture of what the C# language is and what you can accomplish with it. This language review serves as a foundation for discussions in the later chapters.

A Simple C# Program

We start with the simplest C# program you can write, a slight variation on the classic "Hello world!" When compiled, this code prints a text string out to the console.

NOTE

To compile and run the sample programs, the .NET Framework SDK must be installed.

```
class SimpleProgram
{
  public static void Main()
  {
    System.Console.WriteLine("Hello, my name is Inigo Montoya");
  }
}
```

Let's review some of the basics of this program. First, all executable code in C# is contained within a class definition. A class is a template for what an object looks like and how it behaves. Second, notice that C# is syntactically similar to C++. Class and method definitions are enclosed in braces and statements are terminated with semicolons. In fact, most of the operators and the statement formatting of C++ are preserved.

C# can be used to construct component libraries as well as full executable programs. As shown in the preceding program, all executables require a **Main( )** declaration. In contrast, component libraries do not require a **Main( )** declaration. C# doesn't have any built-in or predefined libraries other than those provided by .NET. One of these is **MSCORLib.dll**, which C# provides default access to. It is through this that the **System.Console.WriteLine( )** method, used in the previous listing, writes the specified string to the operating system command console. The **Console** class is found in the System namespace which is why it is prefixed by "System." Namespaces are the way C# segregates the many .NET libraries into reasonable pieces.

The previous code can be compiled using the following command:

```
Csc.exe hello.cs
```

which generates an executable program called **hello.exe**.

A Few More Comments on Main( )

Main( ) can return a value if it's declared as **int** type instead of **void**. A string array can also be specified that will receive command execution parameters passed into the program. The following sample shows a **Main( )** declaration that uses command line arguments. The **Main( )** method includes a declaration for an array of strings called **args**. The **args** array includes any command line parameters passed to the program when it executes.

```
class SimpleProgram
{
  public static int Main(string[] args)
  {
    System.Console.WriteLine("arg 0 is {0}", args[0]);

    return 0;
  }
}
```

The following shows the results of executing the program:

```
C:\Chapter2\Simple Program Fred
arg 0 is Fred
```

Adding a Class to the Simple C# Program

Now that we've built a simple program, let's add a second simple class to it.

```
class SimpleClass
{
  public void SomeMethod()
  {
    System.Console.WriteLine("SomeMethod has been called.");
  }
```

```
}

class SimpleProgram
{
  public static int Main(string[] args)
  {
    SimpleClass sc = new SimpleClass();

    sc.SomeMethod();

    return 0;
  }
}
```

We now have two class declarations. One for our simple class, and one that includes **Main( )**. If we want, we could include the **SimpleClass** declaration within our initial class declaration, which would create nested classes.

Now that we have the basics covered, we move on to C# types and type management.

C# Types and Type Management

Types fall into one of two basic categories: value or reference. *Value type* variables store their data directly and are allocated on the stack. Therefore, the memory for a value type is released when the variable is no longer in scope. *Reference type* variables store a reference or "pointer" to the type's data, which is allocated on the heap. Reference types are garbage collected by the run time when they're no longer referenced. (Garbage collection is discussed in detail in the next chapter.)

In C# there are no special intrinsic types per se. C# does provide special keywords for several of the most common data types but these are essentially shortcuts to data types defined within the Common Language Runtime. For example, the **int** type is an alias to **System.Int32**, the **object** type is an alias to **System.Object** and the **string** type is an alias to **System.String**.

NOTE

Many of the most common run time data types can be accessed using C# keywords rather than specifying the explicit name found in the Common Language Runtime.

Value Types

The following table lists the C# intrinsic value types and what they're aliases for in the .NET run time.

C# Type	Run-time Type	Comments
int	System.Int32	Signed 32-bit integer
uint	System.UInt32	Unsigned 32-bit integer
long	System.Int64	Signcd 64-bit integer
ulong	System.UInt64	Unsigned 64-bit integer
short	System.Int16	Signed 16-bit integer
ushort	System.UInt16	Unsigned 16-bit integer
byte	System.Byte	8-bit unsigned integer
sbyte	System.SByte	8-bit signed integer
float	System.Single	The float type ranges from 1.5×10^{-45} to 3.4×10^{38} with a precision of 7 digits
double	System.Double	The double type ranges from 5.0×10^{-324} to 1.7×10^{308} with a precision of 15–16 digits
decimal	System.Decimal	The decimal type is a 128-bit type that can be used for financial calculations. Decimal can range from 1.0×10^{-28} to approximately 7.9×10^{28} with 28–29 significant digits
bool	System.Boolean	True or false are the only valid values, while conversion to integral types isn't defined
char	System.Char	16-bit Unicode character type

Because these types are derived from **System.Object** (by way of **System.ValueType**), they include base object methods such as **ToString( )**, **GetType( )**, **Equals( )**, and **GetHashCode( )**. The following sample illustrates some of the built-in functionality of the native types.

```
using System;

class TypesSample
{
  public static void Main()
  {
```

```
int a = 5;
byte b = 255;
long c = 5000000;

Console.WriteLine(
    "a is {0}, ToString returns {1}, Type is {2}",
    a, a.ToString(), a.GetType());
Console.WriteLine("b is {0}, Type is {1}", b, b.GetType());
Console.WriteLine("c is {0}, Type is {1}", c, c.GetType());

double d;
d = Math.Pow(2, 100);
Console.WriteLine("d is {0}, Type is {1}", d, d.GetType());

bool e;
e = true;
Console.WriteLine("e is {0}, Type is {1}", e, e.GetType());

    }
}
```

When this code is compiled and run, it displays the following results:

```
a is 5, ToString returns 5, Type is Int32
b is 255, Type is Byte
c is 5000000, Type is Int64
d is 1.2676506002282294E30, Type is Double
e is True, Type is Boolean
```

If you look carefully at the previous code, you can see the native type values and the **Type** object returned from **GetType( )** are passed directly to the **Console.WriteLine( )** method and no special formatting or conversion is required to output a string. Because all types are derived from objects they all support the properties and methods of the **object** class. Therefore, for example, all objects support the **ToString( )** method.

Struct Type

Structs are similar to classes except they are value types designed to implement lean and mean data types. Also, structs don't support inheritance, parameterless constructors, or destructors. Structs do support methods and properties, and they can implement interfaces, static and instance members, and static and instance constructors.

NOTE

All data types that are declared as structs are value types. Value types are allocated on the stack.

Because structs are value types, they're allocated on the stack and are allocated and deallocated efficiently without requiring garbage collection. If the struct is too large, however, passing it as a value parameter can become inefficient compared to a class that simply passes the value of the reference. Therefore, developers should keep structs relatively small, in the region of 16 bytes.

The following example shows a simple struct declaration.

```
using System;

struct SuperType
{
  int m_int;
  public SuperType(int value)
  {
    m_int = value;
  }

  public void Super()
  {
    Console.WriteLine("super type is {0}", m_int);
  }
}

class TestSuperType
{
  public static void Main()
  {
    SuperType si = new SuperType(5);
    si.Super();
  }
}
```

Notice that the implementation of this **struct** occurs within the declaration, rather than in a separate file.

Enumerations

Enumerations define a set of values for data. Enumerations are considered value types and, therefore, instances are allocated on the stack. The base type of an enumerator may be one of **byte**, **sbyte**, **short**, **ushort**, **int**, **uint**, **long**, or **ulong**. The default base type is **int**.

The following sample illustrates the declaration and use of enumerators:

```
using System;

class Enums
{
  enum TheWays
  {
    North,
    South,
    East,
    West
  }

   public static void Main()
   {
      TheWays way = TheWays.West;
      Console.WriteLine("The way is {0}", way);
   }
}
```

This sample produces the following results:

```
The way is West.
```

In addition, enumeration members can specify values explicitly in their declaration and multiple members may share the same value.

```
enum TheWays
{
  North = 1,
  South,
```

```
   East,
   West,
   ToSanJose = West
}
```

When no value is explicitly assigned, the first enumeration member has a value of 0 and each of the other member's value is the value of the previous member plus one. Enumerations are based on the **System.Enum** type.

Reference Types

Now that you know about the basic value types, we move on to reference types. Any class, interface, or delegate (to be defined later in the chapter) and the built-in types of object and string are considered *reference types*. Variables of type reference don't hold the actual data for the object; instead, they hold a reference to the data. The data is allocated on the heap and is automatically garbage collected when it's no longer in use.

To reinforce how reference variables work, consider the following example:

```
using System;

public class SimpleClass
{
  public int x;
  public SimpleClass(int InitialValue)
  {
    x = InitialValue;
  }
}

class EntryPoint
{
  public static void Main()
  {
    SimpleClass c1 = new SimpleClass(1);
    SimpleClass c2;

    Console.WriteLine("c1 is {0}", c1.x);
    c2 = c1;
    c1.x = 2;
```

```
        Console.WriteLine("c2 is {0}", c2.x);
    }
}
```

Note, when **c1** is copied to **c2**, **c1** and **c2** both refer to the same data. Furthermore, changing the data in c1 changes the data in c2 because assigning c2 to c1 results in both variables pointing to the same data storage location in memory. So, the results from executing this program shows **c2** will have a value of 2.

```
c1 is 1
c2 is 2
```

Strings in C#

Even thought **strings** are reference types, they behave a little differently. If we perform the same operation with a **string** as we did with the class earlier, the results are not the same. The following code illustrates the behavior.

```
using System;

class EntryPoint
{
  public static void Main()
  {
    string s1 = "1";
    string s2;

    Console.WriteLine("s1 is {0}", s1);
    s2 = s1;
    s1 = "2";
    Console.WriteLine("s2 is {0}", s2);
    Console.WriteLine("s1 is {0}", s1);
  }
}
```

Here is the output::

```
s1 is 1
s2 is 1
s1 is 2
```

Because string is a reference type, you might expect it to behave exactly as classes do. String is an immutable type, however, its value may not be changed. When the new value is assigned to **s1**, the original data is preserved and the s1 reference is changed to refer to the new string data. While **string** performs well for most string operations, it could prove quite inefficient for intensive in-string manipulations, which is why .NET provides the **System.StringBuilder** class. This class can be used to perform direct modifications to string data when they're needed.

Type Comparisons

Once you have a variable, you inevitably want to compare it with another variable using a comparison operator (==, !=, and so forth). However, you need to be aware that type comparison behavior varies, depending on whether you're comparing two value types or two reference types. Value type comparisons are as you would expect them: the comparison returns true if the values held are identical. Reference type comparisons generally return true if the variables point to the same object. Therefore, the comparison of two objects that contain the same data would not be considered equal.

Interestingly, although **string** is a reference type, as we saw previously with assignment, **string** behaves as a value type. The equality operator is overridden so a string comparison returns true if the values being referred to are identical. **String** also includes a static **Compare** method that can be used to perform case-insensitive comparisons.

Boxing and Unboxing

Boxing is the name of the technique C# uses to convert a value type to **object** (or **System.Object**) and *unboxing* is the name given to the conversion from an **object** back to a value type. Any type, value, or reference can be assigned to an object without an explicit conversion. If the source for the assignment is a value type, C# allocates heap for the value's data, and then assigns the reference to that data to the object. Boxing is used whenever a conversion to **object** is required, either because of explicit assignment or because of parameters being passed to a method call. Unboxing moves a value type from an **object** reference to a value type. Note that conversion rules apply to this assignment. In other words, a value type cannot be unboxed to a different type without an explicit cast.

NOTE

*Converting a value type to **object (System.Object)** is known as boxing.*

The following example illustrates what happens when a value of type **long** is set to **object**, and then the **object** is set back to a **long**. Note, the **long** to **object** conversion occurs implicitly while the **object** to **long** conversion requires a cast. In the latter case, the compiler does not know the original type. However, the run time certainly knows and it validates the conversion before allowing it.

```csharp
using System;

class BoxingSample
{
  public static void Main()
  {
    // First, we do boxing
    object o;
    long Original = 300;

    o = Original;
    Console.WriteLine("o is {0}, type is {1}", o, o.GetType());

    // now we unbox.
    long Copy;
    Copy = (long)o;
    Copy += 5;
    Console.WriteLine("Copy is {0}", Copy);
  }
}
```

Boxing preserves type safety and performance with an object-based type system. Note, also, manual coercing of values into reference types isn't required.

Type Conversions

C# supports both implicit and explicit type conversions. *Implicit conversions* occur without requiring a cast, while *explicit conversions* require a cast. The compiler generates an error if an attempt is made to perform a supported explicit conversion without a cast operator or if an illegal explicit cast is attempted. For a listing of the valid conversions, check the Framework SDK documentation.

The conversion operation can be overridden so your custom classes can provide either implicit or explicit conversions. It is recommended that conversions which can have unintended side effects be overridden explicitly. The explicit cast should be a signal to the user that the conversion may not be perfect. Casting a long to an integer type, for example.

Arrays

C# supports single-dimensioned and multidimensioned arrays. Multidimensioned arrays can be *symmetric* (rectangular) or *jagged,* which is an array of different dimensioned arrays. C# array indexes are 0-based. C# also provides special syntax for initializing arrays.

The following code sample shows simple array declaration, initialization, and use.

```
using System;

class ArraySample
{
  public static void Main()
  {
    int[] ai = {10, 9, 6, 2};

    Console.WriteLine("ai[0] is {0}", ai[0]);
    Console.WriteLine("ai[2] is {0}", ai[2]);
  }
}
```

The previous array initialization is shorthand syntax for the following:

```
int[] ai = new int[] {10, 9, 6, 2};
```

Note, the array size isn't part of the type, so the declaration of **ai** can be set to any size. In the previous case, it's set to a variable width array containing four elements.

System.Array is the base class for all arrays and, therefore, all arrays inherit the functionality of this class. The result is that any array can be iterated on using a **foreach** loop because **System.Array** implements the **ICollection** interface. For example, the integer array previously declared can be iterated on using the **foreach** statement.

```
foreach(int i in ai)
{
  Console.Write("{0}\t", i);
}
```

Some additional methods of interest on **System.Array** include **Sort**, **BinarySearch**, and **Reverse**.

Multidimensioned Arrays

A simple multidimensioned array of strings is shown in the following example:

```
using System;

class ArraySample
{
  public static void Main()
  {
    string[,] ai =
      {{"Allie","10"}, {"Emily","9"},
       {"Johnny","6"}, {"Marian","2"}};

    Console.WriteLine("ai[0] is {0}, {1}", ai[0,0], ai[0,1]);
    Console.WriteLine("ai[2] is {0}", ai[2,0]);
  }
}
```

This sample shows the nesting of array initialization. We have one set of braces for the entire string, and then each of the primary elements of the array has its own initialization statement.

Last, a nonsymmetric, or jagged, array can be declared and used as follows:

```
string[][] activities = {
  new string[] {"piano", "basketball", "drawing"},
  new string[] {"piano", "singing"},
  new string[] {"basketball", "football", "swimming"},
  new string[] {"chess"}
};
```

Because of the object-oriented nature of C# and .NET, only one base array type is required because it can be used to manage an array of any type.

Object-oriented Component Development in C#

C# is designed for the efficient building of object-oriented software components. Software components built in C# are built using classes. Key class constructs including properties, methods, events, and interfaces are defined natively in the C# language and are supported directly by the .NET platform.

In the following section, we first look at how object-oriented programming is implemented in C#. Next, we discuss additional features of classes including the access modifiers, methods, fields, properties, overloading, delegates, and events.

Object-oriented Features of C#

C# is, first and foremost, an object-oriented programming language. The exact definition of what constitutes an object-oriented language is rather diverse. At its core, however, an *object-oriented language* is one that can merge both data and functions into one "black box" known as an *object*.

In this, C# implements object-oriented programming to the fullest extent. In C#, everything from the simplest to the most complex data type is an object. This is because everything derives from **System.Object** (everything except **System.Object**, that is). In fact, if you write a C# class and don't specify any base class, the resulting object still derives from **System.Object**. In other words, declaring class **Employee** without the explicit base class, as in:

```
class Employee
{
   ...
}
```

Is exactly the same as declaring the same class with the **System.Object** specified in:

```
class Employee : System.Object
{
   ...
}
```

Object-oriented principals are used to such an extreme that even hard-coded integers support the methods found on **System.Object**. For example, in C#, you can code **5.ToString( )** and it returns a value. In this case, the string is simply "5" but, nonetheless, the code does compile.

Inheritance

Several other object-oriented characteristics are provided in C#. First is the concept of inheritance. *Inheritance* represents the relationship between two objects—*A* and *B*—such that *B is an A*. For example, if object **A** was an Employee and object **B** was a **Doctor**, then you could create a class hierarchy, such that **B** derived from **A** because a doctor *is a* type of employee. The key in the inheritance relationship is that by deriving object **B** from object **A**, object **B** inherits all the characteristics of **A**. This is known as *extending the base class.* For example, if object **A** has a public function called **Name( )**, then object **B** would also have this function.

```
// build command: csc employee1.csc
//
public class Employee
{
  public void Name()
  {
    //put the code that retrieves the employee name here
System.Console.WriteLine("employee name");
}
}

public class Doctor : Employee
{
}

public class EntryPoint
{
  public static void Main()
  {
    Employee e = new Employee();
    Doctor d = new Doctor();
    e.Name();
    d.Name();
  }
}
```

.NET does not support an advanced form of inheritance called *multiple inheritance.* At least .NET doesn't support multiple inheritance between classes. With a class, objects can*not* be derived directly from more than one class. For example, because a hospital employee could be both an employee and a patient, it could potentially be derived from the two classes **Employee** and **Patient**. However, this data structure isn't possible with either C# or .NET. Chapter 5 includes a full discussion of this potential short fall. But, for the moment, we can consider that .NET does support multiple inheritance with *interfaces,* even if not with classes.

NOTE

There is no class multiple inheritance in C#.

Abstraction

To understand the value of interfaces, which is another key part of the C# language, consider another object-oriented principal, *abstraction.* The purpose of abstraction is to separate the behavior of an object from the implementation of that object. Consider, for example, a function **Call( )** applied to an employee. The implementation for how to call may be reasonably specific to the type of employee being called. For example, to call a doctor, a special answering service is required. This is different from a nurse, which might have a direct-dial hospital extension. Both of these implementations of **Call( )** could be different from the janitor, however. In general, all employees have the function **Call( )**, but there is a difference in how this function is implemented within each employee type. The concept of abstraction separates out the fact that an object has a particular method (**Call( )**) from the implementation of exactly how that method is performed.

In the .NET world, as was the case with the COM paradigm, abstraction is implemented through the use of abstract classes and interfaces.

The defining characteristic of an *abstract class* is that it cannot be instantiated. Therefore, you cannot use the **new** operator on an abstract class. Abstract classes, instead, define the methods and properties a deriving object must implement and the deriving object is what can be instantiated. Abstract classes can support both public and private methods, as well as properties. In addition, an abstract class can include implementation code for its methods, exactly as a normal class does. Just like a normal class, abstract classes don't support multiple inheritance.

An *interface* is a description of the services an object provides to its client. Because there is not much use in exposing services in private methods that clients cannot access, all methods and properties on interfaces are defined as public. The interface defines a contract between the client and the server. Both must abide by its provisions for the client to use the server. If the client doesn't use the same function signatures that the server publicly declares, then the contract between the client and the server is nullified and the call fails. Interfaces are a type of abstract class (although not all abstract classes are interfaces). That is, interfaces are classes that cannot be instantiated directly.

NOTE

All methods and properties on interfaces are defined as public automatically because their purpose is to expose the behavior of the object.

The one other defining characteristic of an interface—and the one that separates it from an abstract class—is that interfaces cannot include any implementation code. In this manner, interfaces only define the metadata, the properties and methods, to be required from any deriving classes.

NOTE

Interfaces cannot have any implementation code. They only contain the property and function signatures that deriving classes require.

Let's return briefly to the concept of inheritance and combine it now with interface abstraction. In .NET, abstraction can be achieved via interfaces from which classes derive to support the behavior that the interface defines. For example, you can define an interface, such as **IEmployee**, and two classes that derive from this interface, such as **Nurse** and **Doctor**. By placing a method called **call( )**on the **IEmployee** interface, you can force the **Nurse** and **Doctor** classes to implement the method.

```
// Build command: csc /t:library Interface1.cs
//
interface IEmployee
{
  string call();
}
class Nurse : IEmployee
{
  public string call()
  {

  }
}
class Doctor : IEmployee
{
  public string call()
  {

  }
}
```

Deriving classes from interfaces is no different than deriving classes from other base classes, except for one important characteristic. In the .NET world, multiple inheritance, although not supported between classes, is supported at the interface level. In other words, it's possible to derive a class from two different interfaces. Taking our earlier hospital employee example, we could create two interfaces—**IEmployee** and **ISalary**—and have the **Doctor** class (or an **IDoctor** interface) derive from both of them. The C# code is shown in the following code listing.

```
// build command: csc interface2.csc
//
namespace HospitalEmployees
{
  using System;

  interface IEmployee
  {
    string call();
  }
  interface ISalary
  {
    void CalculatePay();
  }
  class Nurse : IEmployee, ISalary
  {
    public string call()
    {

    }
    public void CalculatePay()
    {
      Console.WriteLine("Pay the nurse");
    }
  }
  class Doctor : IEmployee, ISalary
  {
    public string call()
    {

    }
    public void CalculatePay()
    {
```

```
        Console.WriteLine("Pay the doctor");
    }
  }
}
```

As already discussed, the example wouldn't compile if both **IEmployee** and **ISalary** were declared as classes, rather than interfaces.

Polymorphism

A third key concept in object-oriented programming is known as polymorphism. Breaking the word down yields the meaning "many forms." Essentially, *polymorphism* is the capability of a single class to behave in multiple ways. Polymorphism can be applied in two ways—inclusion polymorphism and operation polymorphism— both of which are supported by .NET. *Inclusion polymorphism* is directly implemented via interface inheritance or through virtual function overrides. For interface inheritance, given two objects *A* and *B* that are both derived from interface *C*, casting either *A* or *B* to an object of type *C*, and then calling a method on *C*, is possible. In this way, variables of type *C* may refer at run time to two different classes. The call is polymorphic because the exact implementation of the method changes, depending on whether the object cast to *C* is of type *A* or *B*. Let's return to the hospital for another example to help clarify the concept. In this example, we again have the two employee types—doctors and nurses—and both are derived from the interface **IEmployee**. The code follows:

```
// build command: csc Interface3.cs
//
namespace HospitalEmployees
{
  using System;

  interface IEmployee
  {
    string call();
  }
  interface ISalary
  {
    void CalculatePay();
  }
  class Nurse : IEmployee, ISalary
  {
```

```
      public string call()
      {

      }
      public void CalculatePay()
      {
        Console.WriteLine("Pay the nurse");
      }
  }
  class Doctor : IEmployee, ISalary
  {
    public string call()
    {

    }
    public void CalculatePay()
    {
      Console.WriteLine("Pay the doctor");
    }
  }

  class EntryPoint
  {
    static void SendMessage(IEmployee employee)
    {
      employee.Call();
    }

    public static void Main()
    {
      Nurse nurse = new Nurse();
      Doctor doctor = new Doctor();
      SendMessage(nurse);
      SendMessage(doctor);
    }
  }
}
```

In this code, both the Doctor and the **Nurse** are passed to the function
EntryPoint.SendMessage( ). This casts them each to **IEmployee**. However, when

SendMessage( ) is called, the outputs for each function are different because the implementation is different. This is one way in which C# achieves inclusion polymorphism.

Inclusion polymorphism can also be achieved through the use of virtual functions. Given class *C*, which implements a virtual method *V*, classes that derive from *C*, *A*, and *B* can override the virtual function to perform object-specific actions. When *A* or *B* is cast to *C*, calls to *V* from *C* are dispatched to either *A* or *B*. The following example achieves the same inclusive polymorphism result as the previous example, except it uses a virtual method.

```
// build command: csc Employee2.cs
//
namespace HospitalEmployees
{
  using System;

  class Employee
  {
    public virtual void Call()
    {
      Console.WriteLine("calling employee");
    }
  }
  class Nurse : Employee
  {
    public override void Call()
    {
      Console.WriteLine("calling the nurse");
    }
  }
  class Doctor : Employee
  {
    public override void Call()
    {
      Console.WriteLine("calling the doctor");
    }
  }

  class EntryPoint
  {
```

```
    public static void Main()
    {
      Employee e = new Employee();
      e = new Nurse();
      e.Call();
      e = new Doctor();
      e.Call();
    }
  }
}
```

In this example, a particular employee instance, whether it be a **Doctor** or a **Nurse**, is cast to e, which is of type **Employee**. Later on in the **WriteLine( )** code, the **Employee** object e behaves according to the type it was assigned from.

Where the previous example becomes a little hairy is when you consider versioning of the **Employee**. Using the previous example, let's say another assembly, one you don't have source code access to, is providing the **Employee** base class. You decide your derived classes should have a **Shift( )** method to track the employee's shift. So, you place a **Shift( )** method on your Nurse class. The original developer of the **Employee** class might hear of this and decide **Shift( )** would be a good thing for all users of the **Employee** class to have, so they would add this new method to **Employee**. Which **Shift( )** method will be used by your classes derived from **Employee**? By default, your **Nurse** class will hide the **Shift( )** method in the base class. This is true, regardless of the type of the member, be it a field, property, or other member type. If you don't recompile your code, and you use the new **Employee** library as is, your method will hide the method in the base class and virtual dispatching won't be performed. If you rebuild your **Employee**-based components (with no further modification to the code) using the new library, the C# compiler then generates a warning, but still hides the base class. You can eliminate the warning by placing either the **new** or the **override** modifier on your class. Using the **new** keyword continues to hide the base method.

Overloading

The previous samples illustrate inclusion polymorphism. The second type of polymorphism is known as *operation polymorphism*. With operation polymorphism, no inheritance relationship exists between objects. The most common form of operation polymorphism uses overloading. With *overloading,* multiple functions with the same name are created; however, the parameters on each function vary. The result is that a programmer can call the function using the function name and the particular version of the function called is the one that matches the calling signature. Consider the following example:

```
// Build command: csc Employee3.cs
//
namespace HospitalEmployees
{
  using System;

  class Nurse
  {
  }
  class Doctor
  {
  }

  class EntryPoint
  {
    static void Call(Nurse n)
    {
      Console.WriteLine("calling the nurse");
    }
    static void Call(Doctor d)
    {
      Console.WriteLine("calling the doctor");
    }

    public static void Main()
    {
      Nurse nurse = new Nurse();
      Call(nurse);
      Doctor doctor = new Doctor();
      Call(doctor);
    }
  }
}
```

Notice that **Nurse** and **Doctor** no longer derive from **Employee**. Instead, two different **Call( )** functions have been created: one takes **Nurse** as a parameter and the other takes Doctor. The result is Call(nurse) calls static the method void Call(Nurse nurse) and Call(doctor) calls static the method void Call(Doctor doctor). With operation polymorphism (overloading), the multiple forms occur at the function level, rather than at the class level. The same function, defined by its name, takes multiple forms.

Encapsulation

For the same reasons that encapsulation is important to object-oriented programming, it's important to .NET components: *encapsulation* provides a way to bind together code and data, keeping both safe from outside interference or misuse. Through encapsulation, the user of a component need know only how to interact with the component, not how it works. The user of a component doesn't need to know the format and layout of the data within the component and its algorithms. And the user needn't know in what language the module was written. Only the proper method of interfacing with the component needs to be understood. Encapsulation hides the internal workings of a particular class while, at the same time, providing the capability of appropriately exposing the methods and properties the developer chooses.

C# supports four scope modifiers that provide five different ways to declare the scope of a method or property. First, **public** can be used to declare that a method or property is available to all objects, regardless of their relationship to the class containing the method or property. Second, **private** can be used to indicate that only the class that owns the method or property can access the method or property. Third, **protected** is used to scope a property or method, so only the class owning the method or property or any of the classes' decedents can access the property or method. Fourth, **internal** is used to scope a property or method within an assembly only. Internal scope can be used to hide classes from users of an assembly, yet still provide "public" access from within the assembly. Last, **internal protected** methods and properties are only available to the assembly or to derived classes. With the exception of **internal**, these scope rules closely match those provided by C++, once again reflecting C#'s heritage.

NOTE

Encapsulation provides a way to bind together code and data, keeping both safe from outside interference or misuse.

In addition to control over scope, the developer also has control over whether a given class can be derived from using the **sealed** modifier. **Sealed** applies to a class only, and prevents a different class from inheriting it. While there aren't many instances in which it's appropriate, **sealed** can be used to indicate that a class is deprecated or that it provides a special static function.

Class Constructors and Destructors

A class can declare a constructor to initialize itself. Both static and instance-based constructors are supported. *Static constructors* are called automatically when a class is first loaded, while *instance constructors* are called whenever a new instance of the class is created. Constructors can be overridden and overloaded to provide special initializations. The following example illustrates a static constructor and various overloaded instance constructors:

```
// build command: csc ctor.cs
//
namespace CSharpHeadStart
{
  using System;

  class CtorTest
  {
    static CtorTest()
    {
      Console.WriteLine("CtorTest() static constructor");
    }
    public static void MethodA()
    {
      Console.WriteLine("static method MethodA()");
    }
    public CtorTest()
    {
      Console.WriteLine("CtorTest() instance constructor");
    }
    public CtorTest(int IntValue)
    {
      Console.WriteLine("int CtorTest({0})", IntValue);
    }
    public CtorTest(string StringValue)
    {
      Console.WriteLine("string CtorTest({0})", StringValue);
    }
  }

  class EntryPoint
  {
    public static void Main()
```

```
      {
        Console.WriteLine("started");
        CtorTest.MethodA();
        Console.WriteLine("after static method");
        CtorTest ct = new CtorTest();
        CtorTest ct2 = new CtorTest(24);
        CtorTest ct3 = new CtorTest("test");
        Console.WriteLine("ended");
      }
    }
}
```

Executing this code produces the following output:

```
started
CtorTest() static constructor
static method MethodA()
after static method
CtorTest() instance constructor
int CtorTest(24)
string CtorTest(test)
ended
```

Constructor methods are not inherited; so you cannot override a constructor in the base class. The parameterless base class constructor is invoked by default from a derived class unless another constructor is explicitly invoked using the **base** keyword, as shown next.

```
public CtorTest() : base(5)
{
    ...
}
```

If no constructor is defined in a derived class, the base constructor is still called. A static constructor (a constructor declared with the static keyword), is always the first method called on a class, but is only called if the class is used.

Default parameters for the constructor can be supplied by manually invoking an alternate constructor from the constructor method invoked by the client. For example, if the default constructor from the previous sample is modified as follows, then the int overloaded constructor is called prior to this constructor.

```
public CtorTest() : this(5)
{
```

```
   Console.WriteLine("instance constructor called");
}
```

It is a good idea is to locate all initialization in one constructor when overloaded constructors are required. The previous constructor includes the **WriteLine( )** only to illustrate that both constructors are called. Here's the output from the modified sample, showing the int constructor being called twice—once before the default instance constructor and once after:

```
started
CtorTest() static constructor
static method MethodA()
after static method
int CtorTest(5)
CtorTest() instance constructor
int CtorTest(24)
string CtorTest(test)
ended
```

Destructors can be declared to clean up any unmanaged resources used by the class. Destructors are declared using the standard C++ style syntax. A destructor for the previous class is declared as follows:

```
~CtorTest()
{
   Console.WriteLine("finishing up.");
}
```

Unlike C++ destructors, the C# class destructor isn't called immediately after the class instance goes out of scope. Furthermore, the destructor cannot be called explicitly. Instead, the garbage collector calls the destructor at an indeterminate time after all references are removed. Garbage collection and finalization are discussed in further detail in Chapter 3. Chapter 5 discusses the approaches to the problem of the lack of deterministic destruction.

Methods

Methods can take a list of parameters and can also return a value. Methods may either be of type static or instance. Static member methods are available without an instance of the class, while instance methods must be called from an object instance. **Main( )** is a good example of a public static method.

Method Parameters

By default, method parameters are passed by value. If you want to write a function that can change a value and have it remain changed when it returns to the caller, however, you can use the **ref** keyword in the method declaration as follows:

```
public void TestValue(ref ValueClass vc)
```

A value must be set by the caller prior to the method call, otherwise, the C# compiler generates an error. As previously mentioned, changing the data pointed to by a reference data type inside a method call causes the object instance to change and that change remains even after the function returns regardless of whether the ref keyword is used. Therefore, modifications to the object made by the method are made directly to the object itself. If a reference type parameter is declared with the ref keyword, the method can modify the reference value, the pointer. This enables the method to change what a reference is pointing to. The following example illustrates a reference parameter combined with a reference type. It illustrates that when a reference type is passed, the reference itself is modified.

```
// build command: csc refparam.cs
//
using System;

class ValueClass
{
  public int aValue = 1;
}

class SimpleClass
{
  public void TestValue(ref ValueClass vc)
  {
    Console.WriteLine("TestValue: Initial value is {0}", vc.aValue);
    vc.aValue = 2;
    Console.WriteLine("TestValue: Value after is {0}", vc.aValue);

    ValueClass vc2 = new ValueClass();
    vc2.aValue = 22;
    vc = vc2;
```

```
    }
}

class SimpleProgram
{
  public static void Main()
  {
    SimpleClass sc = new SimpleClass();
    ValueClass vc = new ValueClass();

    Console.WriteLine("Main: Value before is {0}", vc.aValue);
    sc.TestValue(ref vc);
    Console.WriteLine("Main: Value after is {0}", vc.aValue);
  }
}
```

If you're used to managing your own memory in languages like C++, you might be ready to pick up the phone, call the authors, and tell them about the object they just dropped on the floor. Before you pick up the phone, remember C# provides automatic garbage collection. The **ValueClass** object reference disconnected in the **TestValue( )** method is cleaned up by the .NET garbage collector.

A special form of reference parameter—output—may also be used. A method indicates that a parameter value will definitely change using the out keyword. Because the parameter definitely changes in the method call, the caller isn't required to initialize an output parameter prior to the method call. However, the method is required to set the value; otherwise, a compile error is generated. The following sample shows use of the **out** parameter modifier combined with a reference type:

```
// build command: csc outparam.cs
//
using System;

class ValueClass
{
  public int aValue = 1;
}

class SimpleClass
{
  public void TestValue(out ValueClass vc)
  {
    ValueClass vc2 = new ValueClass();
```

```
    vc2.aValue = 22;
    vc = vc2;
    Console.WriteLine("TestValue: value is {0}", vc.aValue);
  }
}

class SimpleProgram
{
  public static void Main()
  {
    SimpleClass sc = new SimpleClass();
    ValueClass vc = new ValueClass();

    Console.WriteLine("Main: Value before is {0}", vc.aValue);
    sc.TestValue(out vc);
    Console.WriteLine("Main: Value after is {0}", vc.aValue);
  }
}
```

In summary, initialization of output parameters are the responsibility of the method and initialization of reference parameters are the responsibility of the caller.

Variable Parameter Methods

The params modifier provides support for a variable number of arguments in method calls. All variable parameters must be of a single type. The following sample shows a method that uses params to accept a variable number of objects:

```
// build command: csc params.cs
//
using System;

class SimpleProgram
{
  public static void DumpParameters(params object[] args)
  {
    Console.WriteLine("Dump Parameters: ");
    for(int iArg = 0; iArg < args.Length; iArg++)
    {
      Console.WriteLine("{0}:{1}", iArg, args[iArg]);
    }
  }
```

```
static void Main(string[] args)
{
  DumpParameters("one", "two", 3);
  DumpParameters(2.2, 85, 42, "fred", "barney", "wilma", "betty");
  DumpParameters();
}
}
```

Note, because the variable parameter list is declared as an array, the method call may also take a single array of the appropriate type. This is demonstrated in the following code snippet:

```
object[] SomeParams = {"x", "y", "z", 1, 2, 3};
DumpParameters(SomeParams);
```

Fields

A *field* is defined as any class variable of any type. Although fields may be declared using any of the member accessibility attributes previously defined (public, private, and so forth), the recommendation is that fields only be declared as private member variables. To expose field values, add a property as described in the next section.

Two additional modifiers can be applied to fields. Constant fields can only be modified when they're initialized at class declaration time and these are designated using the **const** modifier. Because of the initialization constraints, const types can be of value type, a string constant, or the special type null. In contrast to constant fields, read-only fields are declared using the **readonly** modifier and are a bit more flexible because the fields can be set inside the class constructor.

Properties

Properties are effectively methods with a built-in pattern for setting and getting a value. Using a built-in pattern establishes a syntax, which is supported and enforced by the compiler and not the developer. Properties don't natively exist in C++ and Java and, therefore, programs written in C++ and Java require custom-style conventions be followed to help ensure readable code.

NOTE

Fields should be declared with a private scope and then the values exposed outside the class using a property.

The following example shows how to declare a property:

```
// Build command: csc properties.cs
//
using System;
class SimpleClass
{
  private int propertyValue = 24;

  public int AProperty
  {
    get
    {
      return propertyValue;
    }
    set
    {
      propertyValue = value;
    }
  }
}

class SimpleProgram
{
  public static void Main()
  {
    SimpleClass sc = new SimpleClass();

    Console.WriteLine("Property initial value: {0}", sc.AProperty);
    sc.AProperty = 5;
    Console.WriteLine("New property value: {0}", sc.AProperty);
  }
}
```

The method invoked when a property is read is the *get accessor*, while the method invoked when a property is modified is the *set accessor*. The get accessor uses the keyword **return** to return the value property to the caller. The set accessor provides the value keyword, which provides access to the assigned value. Property declarations can use all method modifiers including new, virtual, override, or abstract. A read-only property is implemented by not implementing a set accessor.

In addition, C# exposes the property as metadata, which helps make the class libraries easier to use.

> **NOTE**
>
> *A read-only property is implemented by not implementing a set accessor.*

Properties in C# expose similar functionality to fields, but they offer a greater degree of control. Properties are methods invoked when the value of the property is read or modified. This allows a class to further encapsulate its function. Properties are an improvement over plain methods because they provide an explicit syntax and intent for the class implementation, while providing a mechanism for class users that's no different than a field. Although this isn't specifically required, the recommendation is that fields are exposed as properties. This provides maximum protection from future implementation changes to users of the class.

Operator Overloading

C# supports operator overloading of all the standard unary and binary operators, as well as implicit and explicit conversion operators. Operator overloading gives you the opportunity to customize what these operators mean to your class or struct.

The overloadable operators are +, -, !, ~, ++, —, true, false, *, /, %, |, ^, <<, >>, ==, !=, >, <, >=, and <=. No other operators, including the assignment operator can be overloaded. Also note, comparison operators must be overloaded in pairs or groups (<> and == with != for example). The following sample illustrates the implementation of a simple **Vector** type that includes the capability to add and subtract, as well as to compare vectors. The equality operator, (==) and the nonequality operator != are overloaded and an explicit conversion from **int** to **Vector** is provided.

```
// build command: csc vector.cs
//
using System;

public struct Vector
{
    int x;
    int y;
    int z;

    public Vector(int x, int y, int z)
```

```
{
  this.x = x;
  this.y = y;
  this.z = z;
}

public static Vector operator +(Vector v1, Vector v2)
{
  return new Vector(v1.x + v2.x, v1.y + v2.y, v1.z + v2.z);
}
public static Vector operator -(Vector v1, Vector v2)
{
  return new Vector(v1.x - v2.x, v1.y - v2.y, v1.z - v2.z);
}
public static bool operator ==(Vector v1, Vector v2)
{
  return v1.Equals(v2);
}
public static bool operator !=(Vector v1, Vector v2)
{
  return !(v1 == v2);
}
public override bool Equals(object Value)
{
  Vector vectorValue;
  vectorValue = (Vector)Value;
  return ((this.x == vectorValue.x)
    && (this.y == vectorValue.y)
    && (this.z == vectorValue.z));
}
public override int GetHashCode()
{
  return this.x + this.y + this.z;
}

public override string ToString()
{
  return x + "," + y + "," + z;
}

// supply an int to vector conversion
public static explicit operator Vector(int Value)
{
```

```csharp
      return new Vector(Value, Value, Value);
   }
}

class EntryPoint
{
  public static void Main(string[] args)
  {
    Vector v1 = new Vector(1, 1, 1);
    Vector v2 = new Vector(2, 3, 4);
    Vector v3 = v1 + v2;

    Console.WriteLine("v1 is {0}", v1);
    Console.WriteLine("v2 is {0}", v2);
    Console.WriteLine("v3 is {0}", v3);

    Vector v4 = v2 - v1;
    Console.WriteLine("v4 is {0}", v4);

    if(v1 == v4)
    {
      Console.WriteLine("how'd that happen?");
    }
    else
    {
      Console.WriteLine("v1 does not have the same value as v4");
    }

    Vector v5 = (Vector)5;
    Console.WriteLine("v5 is {0}", v5);
  }
}
```

Delegates

In the next two sections, we discuss delegates and events. To aid in this discussion, we use the terms server and client. *Server* is defined as a set of classes as well as the object instances created from those classes, and the *client* is the user of these objects. In most of the examples listed previously in this chapter, the sample classes are the server, and the class we typically call "EntryPoint" is the client.

The standard dictionary definition for *delegate* is "a person acting for another." A *C# delegate* is, effectively, a method acting for another. This level of indirection provides critical functionality when a server needs to call a client.

To help illustrate that point, consider some example applications where delegates can be used. First, consider a data server built to process a special data structure that enables clients to provide custom methods to process the data. The server can be written in advance of, and without prior knowledge of, the custom processing methods. Second, consider a system device driver that receives signals from a device, and then raises events within the application. The device driver cannot be written with prior knowledge of every application that will be interested in device events. Delegates provide a well-defined and rigorous method for clients to register their interest in an event dynamically and long after the device driver is written. And, last, many Windows API functions require callback methods. In a manner similar to events, a library of functions, such as the Windows API, occasionally needs to provide users (or clients) of the library with a way to hook its functionality. Delegates provide a type safe approach for achieving callback functionality in C#.

You need to be concerned with three basic elements when using delegates. First, the delegate *type declaration* identifies the method signature that must be used. Second, *delegate methods* are any function, in any class, that matches the delegate type declaration exactly. Last, the *delegate instance* holds references to methods and is used to invoke the methods. References to the delegate methods are added to the delegate instance. Delegate methods may be static- or instance-based.

In a typical scenario, the server sets up the infrastructure required to invoke the delegate methods, and the client creates the delegate method and tells the server about it. The server object can then execute a delegate method using the delegate instance whenever the server deems appropriate. Essentially, the server says to clients: "If you define a function using this specification and you tell me about it, I'll call it for you whenever it's appropriate." The client says to the server: "Here's a function for you to call as needed. It matches your requirements for a method signature." In fact, the C# compiler ensures the method signature matches.

The following sample shows a delegate declaration and how to use it.

```
// build command: csc delegates.cs
//
namespace CSharpHeadStart
{
  using System;
```

```csharp
// delegate declaration
delegate void CallEmployeeDelegate();

public class Doctor
{
  // delegate method
  public void CallDoctor()
  {
    Console.WriteLine("calling doctor");
  }
}

public class Nurse
{
  // delegate method
  static public void CallNurse()
  {
    Console.WriteLine("calling nurse");
  }
}

public class EntryPoint
{
  public static void Main()
  {
    Doctor doctor = new Doctor();
    // delegate instance
    CallEmployeeDelegate d1 =
      new CallEmployeeDelegate(doctor.CallDoctor);
    d1();

    // second delegate instance
    CallEmployeeDelegate d2 =
      new CallEmployeeDelegate(Nurse.CallNurse);
    d2();

    // third delegate instance
    CallEmployeeDelegate d3 = d1 + d2;
    d3();
  }
}
```

In the previous code, both **Doctor** and **Nurse** provide methods that match the prototype declared by the delegate, but **Doctor** provides an instance method and Nurse provides a static method. Delegate instances **d1** and **d2** are declared and initialized with these method names, so the delegate instances can be used to invoke the methods. Because **Doctor** provides an instance-based implementation, **Doctor** object must be created before its delegate method can be used. The **Nurse.CallMethod( )** can be used directly because it's static. Finally, a third delegate is declared, and **d1** and **d2** are added to it. The delegate supports this because it's a *multicast delegate*. A delegate will be a *multicast delegate* if it is declared as returning void and doesn't have any output parameters. Delegate methods may be combined in a single multicast delegate instance. When the delegate **d3** is invoked, both the **d1** and the **d2** delegate methods are invoked. Delegate methods can be added to and removed from a multicast delegate instance at any time.

Programmers sometimes ask why multicast delegates cannot return a value or output parameters. The reason is pretty straightforward: because the server automatically invokes all delegate methods at once, it has no way to process individual return values.

Events

C# also supports the explicit declaration of events on classes. Events formalize the structure used in the delegate sample previously illustrated. With an event, the intention of the server to be responsible for raising the event is made clear. Events can be implemented as properties with **add** and **remove** accessors. This provides a way to tune the implementation of the event. For example, allocating any resources required to raise the event can be postponed until a listener is added.

The following code implements a simple hospital patient monitoring system. The server class **PatientMonitor** implements an event to be raised whenever the patient needs attention. A parameter is included on the event that indicates whether the situation is an emergency. **Doctor** and **Nurse** classes are implemented to listen for events from the **PatientMonitor** and the **PatientMonitor** includes an internal timer used to simulate patient events. When the timer in **PatientMonitor** fires, the timer's event handler raises the monitor event for the patient.

```
// csc patientmonitor.cs
//
namespace CShartHeadStart
{
  using System;
  using System.Timers;
```

```
/// MonitorDelegate is used to inform clients
/// that a PatientMonitor event has occurred.
/// IsEmergency is True indicates that the event is an emergency.
public delegate void MonitorDelegate(bool IsEmergency);

class PatientMonitor
{
  // private value that indicates
  // an emergency situation
  private bool emergencyFlag;

  // delegate instance that manages
  // listening delegate methods
  private MonitorDelegate monitorEvent;

  // private timer used to automatically
  // trigger patient calls
  private Timer sleepTimer = new Timer();

  // event delegate property that wraps our
  // private delegate instance
  public event MonitorDelegate MonitorEvent
  {
    add
    {
      // We don't bother with the timer
      // unless at least one client is listening
      // If there's more than one client,
      // we still only need one clock.
      if(monitorEvent == null)
      {
        StartMonitorTimer();
      }
      monitorEvent += value;
    }
    remove
    {
      // if all delegates are removed,
      // we can stop the timer
      monitorEvent -= value;
      if (monitorEvent == null)
      {
```

```
        sleepTimer.Enabled = false;
      }
    }
  }


  /// An internal timer is used to simulate
  /// monitor events
  /// In our demo, the monitor goes off every 2 seconds
  /// and alternates between a normal call or an
  /// emergency call
  private void StartMonitorTimer()
  {
    sleepTimer.Tick += new EventHandler(OnTimedEvent);
    sleepTimer.Interval = 2000;
    sleepTimer.Enabled =true;
  }


  /// When the timer Tick event is raised,
  /// we fire our monitor event
  void OnTimedEvent(object source, EventArgs e)
  {
    // Indicate whether this is an emergency
    FireMonitorEvent(emergencyFlag);
    emergencyFlag = !emergencyFlag;
  }


  // FireMonitorEvent fires event delegates if
  // there are any.
  public void FireMonitorEvent(bool IsEmergency)
  {
    Console.WriteLine("Monitor Event!");
    if(monitorEvent != null)
    {
      // Use the private delegate instance to invoke
      // the delegate methods
      monitorEvent(IsEmergency);
    }
  }
}


// The doctor listens for patient monitor events
class Doctor
{
```

```csharp
  public void MonitorEventHandler(bool IsEmergency)
  {
    Console.Write("Doctor, Message From Patient Monitor: ");
    if(IsEmergency)
    {
      Console.WriteLine(" Emergency!");
    }
    else
    {
      Console.WriteLine(" Please Call.");
    }
  }


  // In the constructor for Doctor,
  // we receive a PatientMonitor instance
  public Doctor(PatientMonitor PatientMonitorObject)
  {
    // Add our delegate method to any existing
    PatientMonitorObject.MonitorEvent +=
      new MonitorDelegate(this.MonitorEventHandler);
  }
}

// A nurse listens for patient monitor events
class Nurse
{
  // create a method that can be used as a monitor delegate
  public void MonitorEventHandler(bool IsEmergency)
  {
    Console.Write("Nurse, Message from Patient Monitor:");
    if (IsEmergency)
    {
      Console.WriteLine(" Emergency!");
    }
    else
    {
      Console.WriteLine(" Please call.");
    }
  }
  // In the constructor for Nurse,
  // we receive a PatientMonitor that we need
  // to listen for
  public Nurse(PatientMonitor PatientMonitorObject)
```

```
    {
      // Add our delegate method to any existing
      PatientMonitorObject.MonitorEvent +=
        new MonitorDelegate(this.MonitorEventHandler);
    }
  }

  // Here we create our Doctor and Nurse
  // instances and then we wait for things to happen.
  class EntryPoint
  {
    public static void Main()
    {
      PatientMonitor monitor = new PatientMonitor();
      Doctor doctor = new Doctor(monitor);
      Nurse nurse = new Nurse(monitor);
      // Hold up a bit so we can see
      // the events firing.
      String UserInput = Console.ReadLine();
    }
  }
}
```

Let's review the key points in the sample that relate to events. First, a delegate is declared—**MonitorDelegate**—that specifies the delegate type for the event. Second, the **PatientMonitor** class declares a property and accompanying private field based on this delegate. Third, the **PatientMonitor** class provides a method— **FireMonitorEvent**—which raises the event by calling the delegate. Last, the client classes **Doctor** and **Nurse** implement delegate methods and adds them to the list of delegates on the **PatientMonitor** object. The **PatientMonitor** requires no knowledge of its clients to invoke methods on them. The client methods receive the events and take the appropriate action.

Namespaces in C#

We've ignored these up to now, but namespaces are crucial to any significant development done in C#. We use the **System** namespace frequently in our samples via the **using** keyword as follows:

```
using System;
```

This allows us to type **Console.WriteLine( )** instead of **System.Console.WriteLine( )**. The **System** namespace includes all of the base types for the .NET core runtime library.

Namespaces can also be built hierarchically using dot notation. This allows a single namespace to become quite large by segregating similar classes and interfaces into sub-namespaces. In the previous event sample, a system timer was used to trigger the firing of the event. This came from the **Timer** class, which is in the **System.Timers** namespace. By specifying "**using System.Timers**" we added classes in this namespace into the global namespace enabling us to directly declare a **Timer** object without explicitly using the namespace.

The using keyword can also be used to declare aliases. The alias can represent the namespace or it can represent a class from the namespace. This is handy if you only want a few functions from a particular namespace. Aliases can also be used when some of the types or methods in a namespace collide with existing types or methods. A simple alias declaration is shown in the following example:

```
using con = System.Console;
```

This would allow the following code to be written:

```
con.WriteLine("Hello, my name is Inigo Montoya");
```

Declaring Namespaces

You declare your own namespaces using the **namespace** keyword. Dot notation is also used to define the hierarchy of your namespace. Use of a standard naming convention is recommended so third-party users can more easily digest classes you define. The recommendation is that you prefix any namespace you define with either a company name or a significant product name. Declaration of a namespace is shown in the following sample.

```
namespace SomeCompany.Simple
{
  public class SimpleClass
  {
  }
}
```

Now our **SimpleClass** can be segregated from the vast population of other **SimpleClass** declarations. When someone else comes up with the great idea of

calling a class **Simple**, your users have an out. They declare they're using the
SomeCompany.Simple namespace:

```
using SomeCompany.Simple;
```

Exceptions

The **try, catch**, and **finally** keywords are used to implement exception handling
in C#. All exceptions in C#, including user-defined exceptions, are derived from
System.Exception. Exceptions are explicitly thrown with the **throw** statement.
An unhandled exception terminates a thread or program.

The design of exceptions allows your code to start with general exception handling,
and then be finely tuned based on specific cases you want handled differently.

Exceptions can be nested in that a new exception can be raised while in an
exception handler. Rather than getting lost, the original exception is available via
the **InnerException** property. This enables you to determine if the exception was
thrown from within an exception handler as well as determine what the original
exception was.

Crucial to component development is the clean handling of exceptions, in
particular, handling exceptions among different components from different
providers. The C# exception handling design promotes clean separation without
functional degradation. In other words, your code doesn't require intimate details
of an object to perform effective handling of errors raised by that object.

The following sample illustrates simple error handling:

```
// build command: csc trycatch.cs
//
using System;

class SimpleProgram
{
  public static void Main(string[] args)
  {
    try
    {
      byte a = 10;
      byte b = 0;
```

```
      Console.WriteLine("a/b is {0}", a/b);
      Console.WriteLine("if we haven't thrown yet...");
    }
    catch(Exception e)
    {
      Console.WriteLine("Exception {0} has been caught", e);
    }

    Console.WriteLine("Program ended normally.");
  }
}
```

As soon as an exception is raised, control is transferred directly to the exception handler. No more statements in the **try** block are executed. Also note, no way exists to return control back into the **try** block from the exception. Control can only be returned to some point prior to the **catch** block. So, if a retry attempt is desired, the units of work should be constructed small enough so they can be reexecuted cleanly.

In the following example, we add a **finally( )** block, which is executed regardless of the exit conditions of the **catch** block, and we add an explicit **catch** for divide by 0 in which we "repair" our mistake and reexecute the code.

```
// build command: csc trycatchfinally.cs
//
using System;

class SimpleProgram
{
  public static void Main(string[] args)
  {
    byte a = 10;
    byte b = 0;

ExecuteDivision:
    try
    {
      Console.WriteLine("a/b is {0}", a/b);
      Console.WriteLine("if we haven't thrown yet...");
    }
    catch(System.DivideByZeroException e)
    {
```

```
   // Divide by 0, set b to 1 and retry
   Console.WriteLine("Exception {0} has been caught", e);
   b = 1;
   goto ExecuteDivision;
  }
  catch(Exception e)
  {
    Console.WriteLine("Exception {0} has been caught", e);
  }
  finally
  {
    Console.WriteLine("finally executed");
  }

  Console.WriteLine("Program ended normally.");
 }
}
```

If you find the handler cannot or should not handle the exception, it can be rethrown with the **throw** statement and no parameter.

To control overflow exceptions, the **checked** and **unchecked** operators can be applied to assignment statements. Unchecked statements won't throw on assignment overflow, while checked will. Constant expressions that overflow cause a compile error, regardless of any checked or unchecked setting. By default, runtime overflow resulting from supported conversions won't generate exceptions, that is, they execute in unchecked mode.

Finally, you can define your own exception types. An exception must be derived either from an existing exception or directly from the **System.Exception** class.

Attributes

C# also enables attribute-based programming. This lets you change code behavior and add features just by applying a declarative property to virtually any portion of your code including classes, any of the classes' members (fields, methods, member variables, and so forth), interfaces, assemblies, and even parameters and return values. This functionality was first fully introduced to the COM world through Component Services (COM+). In COM+, adding an attribute like **transaction_required** or **queueable** to a component's IDL automatically inserted transaction support into a component or provided MSMQ functionality. .NET extends this feature significantly and defines a number of standard attributes that can be used to provide functionality, such as serialization, security, and compilation modifications, as well as those previously made available through COM+. Furthermore, attributes don't require another distinct language (such as COM required IDL) because they can be coded inline with the original source. Some of the standard attributes used for interoperability are reviewed in Chapter 6.

NOTE

Many of the attributes included with the .NET framework are interpreted at compile time and change the MSIL generated.

In addition to the standard attributes provided by the .NET Framework, you can create your own custom attributes. *Custom attributes* provide additional metadata that can be embedded into your class and examined at run time. Custom attributes don't provide the same level of functionality that many of the standard attributes do. For example, you cannot create custom attributes that affect how your code will be compiled or interpreted by the CLR. Instead, these attributes become meaningful through the use of reflection code that's written to interpret and respond to them at runtime. The result is they still provide a powerful medium for extending functionality. A full discussion of how to create and use custom attributes appears in the following chapter.

NOTE

Unlike standard attributes, you cannot create custom attributes that affect code compilation or that may be interpreted automatically by the CLR.

Indexers

C# indexers provide a way to access classes or properties (usually a specialized collection of objects) using standard array index syntax. Indexers are implemented through get and set accessors for the [] operator. The following sample shows a simple implementation using an integer index:

```
// build command: csc indexers.cs
//
using System;
```

```
class IntIndexer
{
  private static int[] SomeData = {0, 1, 2, 3, 4, 5};
  public int this [int Index]
  {
    get
    {
      try
      {
        return SomeData[Index];
      }
      catch
      {
        return 0;
      }
    }
    set
    {
      try
      {
        SomeData[Index] = value;
      }
      catch
      {
        ;
      }
    }
  }
  public int Length
  {
    get
    {
      return SomeData.Length;
    }
  }
}

public class TestIndexer
{
```

```
public static void Main()
{
  // test the integer index
  IntIndexer someints = new IntIndexer();
  someints[0] = 24;
  someints[5] = 17;
  someints[86] = 12;

  for (int i = 0; i<someints.Length; i++)
  {
    Console.WriteLine("Element #{0} = {1}", i, someints[i]);
  }

  Console.WriteLine("Element 86 is {0}", someints[86]);
}
}
```

In the previous example, we implemented the accessor so the class handles invalid array access automatically. The **get** returns 0 on any error and the set simply ignores the setting on any error. This class isn't recommended for real-world deployment, but what you should glean from this is indexers provide a technique for implementing special array type access—either virtual access to data built on-the-fly or for wrapping a special resource you might not want to load into memory prior to providing users access. A gigabyte-large log file, for example, might take a significant amount of time to load.

Indexers and properties are similar, but some significant differences exist. Indexers must be instance-based, that is, they cannot be static. The get and set accessors are invoked as methods with the parameter list specified in the indexer declaration. The set accessor still has the additional implicit value parameter.

The index parameters can be any type, including strings or objects. If more than one parameter is specified, then the indexer simulates multidimensional access as well. A good idea is to implement the **IEnumerable** interface when implementing an indexer, so that client can use **foreach** to iterate the members. Note, the value provided by the index access isn't a real variable, so an indexer reference cannot be passed directly as a **ref** or **out** parameter to a method.

Finally, just because you can, doesn't necessarily mean you should. Indexers should be reserved for those cases where accessing a class by index makes sense, and where standard array and collection techniques aren't appropriate

Writing Unsafe Code

In addition to the type safety and automatic garbage collection support C# and .NET provide, C# also enables you to write code that directly manipulates memory. Any code marked unsafe allows pointers to be declared and memory to be directly accessed. Memory allocated during unsafe mode is fixed by default, meaning it won't be touched by the garbage collector. This, of course, means you're responsible for cleaning up the memory when you no longer need it. In addition, the fixed keyword can be used to temporarily pin memory managed by the garbage collector. This gives your unsafe code direct access to memory that's managed in safe mode.

The following is a short sample that shows the basic use of the unsafe and fixed keywords. The unsafe keyword is used to mark a method or a property, while the fixed keyword wraps statements using a pointer to managed memory. The fixed keyword can only be used within a procedure or method marked as unsafe.

```
// build command: csc /unsafe unsafe.cs
//
using System;

class EntryPoint
{
  unsafe static void AdjustBytes(byte[] ByteArray)
  {
    fixed (byte* pByte = ByteArray)
    {
      *(pByte + 3) = 99;
      *(pByte + 5) = 99;
      *(pByte + 7) = 99;
    }
  }

  public static void Main()
  {
    byte[] myByteArray = {0, 1, 2, 3, 4, 5, 6, 7, 8, 9};

    AdjustBytes(myByteArray);

    Console.Write("Array contents: ");
    foreach(byte aByte in myByteArray)
```

```
    {
        Console.Write(" {0}", aByte);
    }
  }
}
```

Another unsafe feature provided is **stackalloc**. **Stackalloc** is used to allocate a block of memory off the stack. Use of **stackalloc** is restricted to local variables of unmanaged type in a procedure already declared **unsafe**. So, nothing drastic in terms of memory management is provided here. Stack allocated memory is released along with all other values on the stack when the scope of execution changes.

Documenting Code Using XML

We have one last point to discuss in this review of the C# language. The C# compiler includes a **/doc** parameter that generates an XML file, which documents your classes based on tags you place in code comments. If you adjust your header comment style to include these XML style comments, the C# compiler generates a document for you.

A brief example of the commenting style is included in the following sample. Comment lines that contain the XML tags must begin with three slashes instead of the customary two, and the tags must be placed immediately prior to the type or member being documented. After that, it's only a matter of including the appropriate XML tag. The tag varies based on the type being documented. **<remarks></remarks>** is used for classes or types, while **<summary></summary>** is used for type members. Several others can be included for various items, such as return values **<return>**, parameters **<param>**, describing an example **<example>**, and two forms for example code: **<c>** for one line or short code, and **<code>** for multiple lines of code. Refer to the documentation for a full listing of all the tags.

The following text documents the **MonitorDelegate** used for the **PatientMonitor** class from the previous example:

```
/// <summary>
/// MonitorDelegate is used to inform clients
/// that a PatientMonitor event has occurred.
/// <param name="IsEmergency">
```

```
/// True indicates that the event is an emergency.
/// </param>
/// </summary>
public delegate void MonitorDelegate(bool IsEmergency);
```

When the /doc compiler option is used, an XML file is generated that contains all the comments in the file in a **<doc>** tag. The **<assembly>** and **<member>** tags are generated automatically by the compiler. A **<member>** tag is generated for each class or member that includes a documentation tag. If the class or member doesn't include a tag, it won't be included in the output. Therefore, for a document to be complete, every member must be tagged. This applies to private, as well as public members. If a private member is tagged, it also shows up in the generated document.

The following is the XML generated for the previous document lines:

```
<?xml version="1.0"?>
<doc>
    <assembly>
        <name>PatientMonitor_doc</name>
    </assembly>
    <members>    <members>
        <member name="T:CShartHeadStart.MonitorDelegate">
            <summary>
            MonitorDelegate is used to inform clients
            that a PatientMonitor event has occurred.
            <param name="IsEmergency">
            True indicates that the event is an emergency.
            </param>
            </summary>
        </member>
    </members>
</doc>
```

The compiler generates a **<member>** tag for each documented member. In our sample, only the **MonitorDelegate** is documented. The name attribute of the **<member>** tag identifies the name and type of the member. In this case, we see a *T* for Type. Other possible member types include *N, F, P, M,* and *E* for namespace, field, property, method, and event, respectively. An exclamation point ("!") is used to indicate a format error. The text following the ! provides information on the error.

C# Coding Style

Before we move on to the next chapter, we want to make a quick note on coding style. Coding style standards are a good thing. In fact, everyone should have one! All kidding aside, this is a fairly critical issue when it comes to the reuse of components as well as building reusable class hierarchies. Following well-understood coding standards can make the class libraries you develop more usable by coworkers, third-party developers of your public classes, as well as anyone given the task of maintaining the class hierarchy.

The .NET Framework SDK includes the .NET Framework Developer Specifications, which includes the .NET Framework Design Guidelines. We've made a reasonable attempt to follow the guidelines described in that specification in this book. Here are some of the main points in the C# style guide:

▶ Use PascalCasing for just about everything including classes, interfaces, enumerations, methods, and properties. PascalCasing capitalizes the first letter of each word in a name, and multiple word names are simply appended together with no separator character.

▶ Use camelCasing for local method variables or private class variables. camelCasing lowercases the first word of a name while subsequent words are uppercased. Again, multiple word names are simply appended together.

▶ Interfaces should always start with an I.

▶ Use nouns for class names and verbs for method names. For example, class **PatientMonitor** and public method **FireMonitorEvent( )**.

We highly recommend reviewing the design guidelines for yourself before you get deep into creating your own C# code.

CHAPTER 3

.NET, the Operating Environment for C#

IN THIS CHAPTER:

Microsoft IL

.NET Building Blocks

Building Modules and Assemblies

Robust Version Control

Built-in Metadata

Cross-language Interoperability

Common Language Specification

Common Type System

Object-oriented

Delegation and Events

Memory Management Through Garbage Collection

Thread Synchronization

The previous chapter provided an overview into the language constructs of C#. As you saw, C# is a powerful language that includes all the major features demanded of modern-day computer languages. C# will appeal to both new and experienced programmers because it not only captures the ease of use that accompanies Visual Basic, but also makes the power of C++ readily available. Although C# provides a syntax that's rich and relatively easy to use, the syntax isn't the core of the language. Rather, the majority of C# features are enabled through the underlying architecture of the language.

As already mentioned, C# is built on the .NET Framework and this is the framework that enables almost all the features found in C#. At its core, C# is a language designed to fully expose the .NET Framework. Therefore, to garner a good understanding of C#, you need to understand the underlying architecture. In this chapter, we examine the .NET Framework and see how it enables many of the features discussed in the previous chapter.

Given the breadth of the .NET Framework, investigating it entirely within one chapter isn't possible. Instead, the focus is on the following areas:

▶ Microsoft IL

▶ .NET Building Blocks

▶ Version Control

▶ Built-in Metadata

▶ Memory Management Through Garbage Collection

Microsoft IL

The key to the .NET Framework is found in MSIL. As introduced in Chapter 1, IL replaces the binary standard for intermodule communication previously established by COM. In other words, various modules can interoperate via IL. Furthermore, through IL, it becomes possible to commingle the various .NET languages.

IL code is a CPU-independent language that usually only gets converted to machine-specific execution instructions at runtime. IL code isn't simply the product of code run through a precompiler, but not yet compiled and optimized into native machine code. When a managed application begins, the Common Language Runtime gets invoked, takes the compiled IL code, and runs it through the JIT compiler to create native machine code. (See the accompanying in-depth box for details on exactly how the CLR gets loaded.) The IL language is such an integral part of the .NET technology, you can view the IL code of an assembly (without having the original source code) by loading up a .NET file into the managed code disassembler, **ILDasm.exe**.

For example, if you compile the **Hello.cs** file from Chapter 2 into a module called **Hello.exe**, you can then load it into **ILDasm.exe** using the following command:

```
ILDasm.exe Hello.exe
```

This launches **ILDasm.exe** as shown in Figure 3-1, by which you can browse your IL code.

The first item in the tree shows the assembly manifest, discussed later on in the chapter. After the manifest come all the classes, data types, and enumerations within the opened module. If you double-click any of these items, a second dialog box appears that contains the IL code associated with the selected object. For example, double-clicking the Main node displays the following set of IL instructions:

```
.method private hidebysig static void Main() il managed
{
  .entrypoint
  // Code size       11 (0xb)
  .maxstack  8
  IL_0000:  ldstr      "Hello, my name is Inigo Montoya"
  IL_0005:  call       void [mscorlib]System.Console::WriteLine(class
System.String)
  IL_000a:  ret
} // end of method SimpleProgram::Main
```

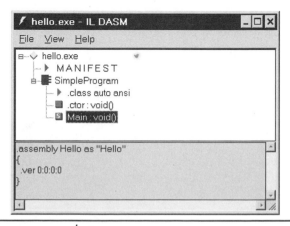

Figure 3-1 *ILDasm.exe screen shot*

The first instruction, IL_000, loads the string "Hello, my name is Inigo Montoya". The next line calls the **System.Console** class, which is located in **mscorlib**. Finally, the function returns at instruction IL_000a.

Note, you can use **ILDasm.exe** to examine more than just your own classes. In fact, the entire .NET library of objects can be opened and inspected. To see that a value type is ultimately derived from **System.Object**, therefore, all you need to do is open the **mscorlib.dll** assembly and browse down to the **System.ValueType** class. The following shows the declaration:

```
.class public auto ansi serializable ValueType
       extends System.Object
{
} // end of class ValueType
```

As you can see by the fact that the IL code can be shown using **ILDasm.exe**, IL code is an integral part of the released module, not simply an intermediate state of your code during compilation. IL is a complete language that includes instructions for memory management, exception handling, control flow, and mathematical operations, along with initializing and calling methods on objects.

How the CLR Gets Loaded

At this point, you've seen how integral IL code is to the entire .NET architecture and, in Chapter 1, what the purpose is of the CLR. What you haven't seen is how the CLR gets loaded when an executable is run. To do this, rerun **ILDasm.exe**, except this time, use the **/header** and **/text** options shown in the following:

```
ILDasm.exe Hello.exe /text /header
```

This opens a different window with a listing of the entire disassembled executable. Alternatively, you can dump the output to a file using the **/out=<filename>** option in place of the previous **/text** option. A listing of most of the **ILDasm.exe** options can be retrieved with the **/?** as you would expect. The resulting output from the previous command is shown in the following lengthy listing (a few line feeds were inserted for formatting purposes).

```
//  Microsoft (R) .NET Framework IL Disassembler.
//  Version 1.0.2204.21
//  Copyright (C) Microsoft Corp. 1998-2000
```

```
// PE Header:
// Subsystem:                         00000003
// Native entry point address:        0000234e
// Image base:                        00400000
// Section alignment:                 00002000
// File alignment:                    00000200
// Stack reserve size:                00100000
// Stack commit size:                 00001000
// Directories:                       00000010
// 0         [0        ] address [size] of Export Directory:
// 2300      [4b       ] address [size] of Import Directory:
// 4000      [2d8      ] address [size] of Resource Directory:
// 0         [0        ] address [size] of Exception Directory:
// 0         [0        ] address [size] of Security Directory:
// 6000      [c        ] address [size] of Base Relocation Table:
// 0         [0        ] address [size] of Debug Directory:
// 0         [0        ] address [size] of Architecture Specific:
// 0         [0        ] address [size] of Global Pointer:
// 0         [0        ] address [size] of TLS Directory:
// 0         [0        ] address [size] of Load Config Directory:
// 0         [0        ] address [size] of Bound Import Directory:
// 2000      [8        ] address [size] of Import Address Table:
// 0         [0        ] address [size] of Delay Load IAT:
// 2008      [48       ] address [size] of COM+ Header:

// Import Address Table
//     mscoree.dll
//              00002000 Import Address Table
//              0000233e Import Name Table
//              0        time date stamp
//              0        Index of first forwarder reference
//
//                    0  _CorExeMain

// Delay Load Import Address Table
// No data.
// CLR Header:
// 72          Header Size
// 2           Major Runtime Version
// 0           Minor Runtime Version
// 1           Flags
```

```
// 6000001   Entrypoint Token
// 2064       [29c       ] address [size] of Metadata Directory:
// 2064       [0         ] address [size] of Resources Directory:
// 0          [0         ] address [size] of Strong Name Signature:
// 0          [0         ] address [size] of CodeManager Table:
// 0          [0         ] address [size] of VTableFixups Directory:
// 0          [0         ] address [size] of Export Address Table:
// 0          [0         ] address [size] of Precompile Header:
// Code Manager Table:
//   default
// VTableFixup Directory:
// No data.
// Export Address Table Jumps:
// No data.

.subsystem 0x00000003
.corflags 0x00000001
.assembly extern mscorlib
{
  .originator = (03 68 91 16 D3 A4 AE 33 )  // .h.....3
  .hash = (52 44 F8 C9 55 1F 54 3F 97 D7 AB AD E2 DF 1D E0
          F2 9D 4F BC )                      //
RD..U.T?.........O.
  .ver 1:0:2204:21
}
.assembly Hello as "Hello"
{
  // --- The following custom attribute is added automatically,
  // --- do not uncomment
  //  .custom instance void
  //     [mscorlib]System.Diagnostics.DebuggableAttribute::.ctor(
  //     bool, bool) = ( 01 00 00 01 00 00 )
  .hash algorithm 0x00008004
  .ver 0:0:0:0
}
.module Hello.exe
// MVID: {E3676EA1-C54C-49A3-967E-F84776D6A436}
.class private auto ansi SimpleProgram
       extends [mscorlib]System.Object
{
  .method private hidebysig static void Main() il managed
```

```
   {
     .entrypoint
     // Code size       11 (0xb)
     .maxstack  8
     IL_0000:  ldstr   "Hello, my name is Inigo Montoya"
     IL_0005:  call    void [mscorlib]System.Console::WriteLine(
       class System.String)
     IL_000a:  ret
   } // end of method SimpleProgram::Main

   .method public hidebysig specialname rtspecialname
           instance void .ctor() il managed
   {
     // Code size       7 (0x7)
     .maxstack  8
     IL_0000:  ldarg.0
     IL_0001:  call    instance void
[mscorlib]System.Object::.ctor()
     IL_0006:  ret
   } // end of method SimpleProgram::.ctor

} // end of class SimpleProgram

//*********** DISASSEMBLY COMPLETE ***********************
```

The interesting part about this listing is the top portion that contains header information, specifically the first address listing that appears immediately below the **// PE Header** line. This listing points to how the CLR gets loaded. First, is the image base address, which is set to **00400000**. This indicates the location of the executing code. Next, comes the native entry point address at **0000234e**. This indicates that the first instruction occurs at an offset of 234e from the image base. In other words, the first instruction is at **0040234e**.

If you load the executable into the debugger and look at the assembly code, you see the instruction at **0040234e** is a **jmp** instruction to **00402000**. Close examination of the **Import Address Table** section of the previous disassembly reveals that address **00402000** (**00400000** plus the **00002000** offset) is the location of **mscoree.dll** and **_CorExeMain** can be found at this location. In this manner, the CLR is called into the execution environment.

.NET Building Blocks

You know now the fundamental element of managed code is IL. In this section, you see what IL code is used to create. Two important items in the area of .NET software need to be defined in the context of building software made up of components, as discussed in Chapter 1. The first is a module and the second is the assembly.

Modules

A module is a formalization of a term that's already been used repeatedly throughout this book. In the .NET Framework, a *module* is a portable executable file, either a DLL or an EXE, which contains the definition of one or more data types (usually classes) along with their code that conforms to the Common Object File Format used for executables. IL is the fundamental element that makes up the functionality of a module.

NOTE

In the .NET Framework, a module is a portable executable file, either a DLL or an EXE, which contains the definition of one or more data types (usually classes) along with their code.

Assemblies

Modules cannot function independently, however. Modules are combined together into units called *assemblies,* which contain a combination of modules, resource files, and metadata to make a unit of the required files. The assembly refers to a "logical" DLL or application that may be composed of more than one physical file/module. In other words, creating an assembly does *not* combine separate physical modules into one file but, instead, it defines a logical unit that needs to be deployed as a package and managed as a unit by the .NET system even though it's made up of separate modules.

Furthermore, modules aren't the smallest versioning unit available. Once created, the entire assembly is marked with a version number and no versioning unit is smaller than an assembly. Therefore, if one module within an assembly is targeted to work with a second module inside the assembly, then that's the module it works with. Developers won't replace the targeted module with a newer version and place it within the same assembly any longer. Instead, they'll create an entirely new assembly.

NOTE

Assemblies define the discrete unit of deployment, reuse, and versioning. No versioning unit is smaller than an assembly.

Essentially, three types of assemblies exist. The first two types are executables: either console-based or Windows-based. Each of these can start a Win32 process. The last type is a library. A *library* provides a set of services that can be accessed by other assemblies, but a library cannot execute on its own because it doesn't form a valid Win32 executable.

Assemblies can be combined together into applications, but the basic building block for a released application is still the assembly, not the individual modules used to create the assembly. As such, assemblies define the discrete unit of deployment, reuse, and versioning.

Application Domains

.NET provides an additional level of process breakdown that is smaller than a process, but larger than a thread. This is known as an application domain. An *application domain* is used to define a level of isolation for a program without having to consume the resources required for a process. In the past, applications were typically isolated from each other by each being placed into a separate process. This prevents them from corrupting each other's memory and generally limits one application from adversely affecting another. In addition, application isolation provides for varying security restrictions and independent application debugging.

The introduction in .NET of application domains provides similar isolation without the overhead that multiple processes require. Because IL code can be analyzed at runtime, you can determine whether code is type safe, as well as provide a boundary for faults, so that errors will only affect a particular application domain and not an entire process. The result is this: what previously required multiple Win32 processes can now be combined into one process, but divided into multiple application domains.

For all practical purposes, an application domain can be thought of as an individual process in the traditional sense. Each application domain can have its own configuration file and, at runtime, each instance of a particular application domain can have its own data segment. For example, class static variables have their own instance if the same assembly were loaded into two different applications domains within the same Win32 process. Furthermore, interprocess communication invokes a proxy, so no direct calls occur from one domain into another. However, because the calls from one application domain don't have to cross Win32 process boundaries, the calls can be more efficient. Finally, each application domain can run under its own set of privileges or permissions.

Building Modules and Assemblies

As you learned in Chapter 2, you can build an assembly using the C# compiler, **csc.exe**. In each of these examples, only one module was in each assembly. In this section, you learn more about the C# compiler options used to create modules and reference them within assemblies.

By default, the C# compiler creates an assembly, rather than a module. If you want to create a module, you need to use the **/t:module** option where **/t** is short for **/target**. For example, if you had two files—**employee.cs** and **patient.cs**—to compile into a module, you would use the following command line:

```
csc.exe /t:module employee.cs patient.cs
```

or

```
csc.exe /t:module /out:hospital.mod employee.cs patient.cs
```

The addition of the **/out** option enables you to specify what the target file will be. If, however, no target filename is specified, then the name is generated from the name of the first file in the list of files being compiled. Therefore, in the first example, the compiled file will be **employee.dll**, whereas in the second example, **hospital.mod** is explicitly specified. By default, a DLL file extension is used for modules and libraries. (Remember, the difference between a module and that a library is a library is a .NET assembly. In other words, a library contains the additional version and other header information required by an assembly.)

Once you create several modules, you'll want to combine them into an assembly. You can do this using the C# Compiler if you still have any uncompiled files. To reference any modules you already created, use the **/addmodule** option, as follows:

```
csc.exe /addmodule:employee.dll patient.cs
```

On the other hand, if you have no more remaining code and, instead, you want to combine all the existing modules into an assembly, use the **Al.exe** tool. For example, to combine two modules—**employee.dll** and **patient.dll**—into a library called **Hospital.dll**, you use the following:

```
Al.exe /out:Hospital.dll employee.dll patient.dll
```

Note, the resulting file, **Hospital.dll**, still needs to be distributed with the **employee.dll** and **patient.dll** DLLs because, as previously stated, creating an assembly doesn't combine the modules into one file. In the previous command, a library was created. When building an executable, you need to specify one additional option, which is the name of the main function. If, for example, we included the main function inside a class called **EntryPoint** within a namespace **Hospital**, then we could build the **Hospital.exe** file as follows:

```
Al.exe /t:exe /out:Hospital.exe employee.dll patient.dll
  /main:Hospital.EntryPoint.Main
```

Note the addition of the target option **/t:exe**. Without this, a library would be created by default. If you don't include the **/main** when you specify **/t:exe**, the assembly will fail to build.

Robust Version Control

Because assemblies are the smallest versioning unit of an application, we can assume additional information about the assembly version is stored in the assembly. This data forms part of what is known as the *assembly manifest,* which contains metadata embedded into an assembly. Most of the information relates to file and version information. To understand this, let's examine the manifest of the **HospitalSystem.exe** assembly built in the previous section, "Building Components and Assemblies." The following shows a listing of this manifest.

```
.module extern employee.dll
.file employee.dll
```

```
        .hash = (10 F2 7B EB 95 7F 76 07 22 6D 6F FD C7 47 BB D5
            8A 1D BD 8C )   // ..{...v."mo..G..
.file patient.dll
        .hash = (D8 E5 0B 15 0C 73 FE F4 D3 EE A2 0F DF 7E CF BF
                DA B0 74 15 )   // .....s.......~....t.
.assembly extern mscorlib
{
    .originator = (03 68 91 16 D3 A4 AE 33 )   // .h.....3
    .hash = (52 44 F8 C9 55 1F 54 3F 97 D7 AB AD E2 DF 1D E0
            F2 9D 4F BC )   // RD..U.T?..........O.
    .ver 1:0:2204:21
}
.assembly HospitalSystem as "HospitalSystem"
{
    // --- The following custom attribute is added
    // automatically, do not uncomment -------
    // .custom instance void
[mscorlib]System.Diagnostics.DebuggableAttribute::.ctor(bool,
        bool) = ( 01 00 00 01 00 00 )
    .hash algorithm 0x00008004
    .ver 0:0:0:0
}
.module HospitalSystem.exe
// MVID: {7FFEF80F-DF2B-4E55-99FC-3F3F6CFE8134}
```

In this listing, you can see both of the key purposes to the manifest data. The first purpose is to point to a list of all the modules included in the assembly. Notice that to point to a file requires more than simply the filename. In fact, even a combination of the filename and the version number isn't sufficient. (In the previous listing, only **mscore.lib** has a version number because it's the only assembly; modules don't have version numbers.) In addition, the manifest includes a hash that uniquely identifies the linked module or assembly. If you recompile **HospitalSystem.exe**, you see the hash for **Alarm.mod** doesn't change. If you recompile the **Alarm.mod**, the referenced module, and then recompile **HospitalSystem.exe**, however, the hash value changes. The point is this: the manifest uniquely identifies the module used and changing the module changes the identification. If the referenced module was changed or recompiled, it would be possible to tell. Having a listing of external files isn't unique to assemblies; modules also contain these references to indicate what their dependencies are.

The additional metadata an assembly contains beyond a module is the portion within the assembly section, as shown in the following relisted code:

```
.assembly extern mscorlib
{
  .originator = (03 68 91 16 D3 A4 AE 33 )  // .h.....3
  .hash = (52 44 F8 C9 55 1F 54 3F 97 D7 AB AD E2 DF 1D E0
          F2 9D 4F BC )  // RD..U.T?..........O.
  .ver 1:0:2204:21
}
```

By default, the version number for an assembly, when it isn't explicitly specified, is 0:0:0:0. The number is broken down into four parts as follows: <Major>:<Minor>:<Build>:<Revision>. Although missing by default, the version can be set explicitly using an attribute, as the following shows.

```
[assembly: System.Runtime.CompilerServices.AssemblyVersion("1.0.*")]
```

Because the **AssemblyVersion** is an attribute of the assembly, it needs to be placed at a global location within a file and not inside a namespace. If you're using Visual Studio.NET to generate your project, you'll notice it automatically creates an **assembly.cs** file that contains several different assembly properties for you. The advantage of this is all your assembly information will be kept in one file.

Notice in the example where only two digits are specified, the third is simply a star, and the fourth is missing altogether. The star in this location indicates that the build number and revision should be automatically generated. The generated build number will be the number of days since January 1, 2000, and the generated revision will be the number of seconds since midnight. You can also include the build number explicitly and have the revision generated (based on the number of seconds again).

For the CLR to load a referenced module or assembly, it simply uses the filename contained in the assembly and searches for the referenced file in the same directory as the assembly or any child directory. Given this scenario, however, version information becomes irrelevant.

NOTE

For the CLR to load a referenced module or assembly, it uses the filename contained in the assembly and, by default, searches for the referenced file in the same directory or child directory as the application.

Forcing a referenced assembly to be included in the same directory is rather restrictive. It works well if you developed all the modules within the assembly, but it can become a problem otherwise. If 20 different applications are on a computer and they all reference the same file, it seems rather pointless for them all to have their own copies of all files included in an assembly. This helps considerably in solving the various versioning problems, however, because it's unlikely another vendor would override the files you distribute in your own directory. Therefore, the files you distribute are the ones loaded by your application, even if a second application on the same system uses different versions of the same files.

NOTE

The advantage of placing an assembly in the same directory as an application is that simply copying the files can deploy the application. No registration is required.

Even with the relatively cheap cost of disk space, however, there seems little reason to waste resources unnecessarily by forcing each application to install its own copy of a common file. And what happens when you want to apply a patch? Fortunately, two other ways exist of deploying your software without forcing it all to be in the same directory. The first is to specify the location of an assembly using a configuration file. A *configuration file* is an XML file included in the same directory as the application. The name of the file should be the same as the name of the executable, except it should have a CFG extension. An example of such a file follows.

```
<?xml version ="1.0"?>
<Configuration>
  <Assemblies>
    <CodeBaseHint Name=" HospitalInterfaces"
      Originator="BA 91 94 D4 9A A5 17 2F"
      Version="1:2:409:34237"
      CodeBase="c:\CSharpHeadStart\HospitalInterfaces.dll"/>
  </Assemblies>
</Configuration>
```

In addition to providing the capability of having multiple versions of the same file on a computer, both the solutions previously mentioned (placing the assembly in the same directory or referencing it with a configuration file) have another strong advantage: they both can be deployed by simply copying the files on to the computer. There's no need to run some special utility to register them, as was required for COM modules.

Although configuration files may help in reducing the number of duplicate files installed on a system, to expect users to create configuration files manually that point to the location they happened to select for installing a component is unacceptable. The configuration file solution exists more for the benefit of system administrators who are attempting to repair an application, enabling them to specify explicitly where a component is located. A different solution is still needed for deploying a shared assembly.

The third solution is specifically designed for components to be shared by multiple applications. If you're deploying such a file, you want to deploy it using the **gacutil.exe** utility. This utility "registers" the file with the system, so it can be located by the CLR. The GAC in **gacutil.exe** stands for Global Assembly Cache and is the location where shared assemblies are placed and registered. You can get a listing of all the assemblies on your system by executing **gacutil.exe –l** on the command line. In addition, it can be viewed at your <winnt>\assembly\GAC directory.

One additional step must be performed before your application can be registered with **gacutil.exe**: you need to sign your application. The easiest way to do this is to create a signature key file using the following command:

```
sn -k CSharpHeadStart.snk
```

You then need to reference this file from within one of your source files, **assembly.cs** by convention. This is done with the following code:

```
[assembly: AssemblyDelaySign(false)]
[assembly: AssemblyKeyFile("CSharpHeadStart.snk")]
```

After compiling the assembly, you can then register it using **gacutil.exe**, as previously described.

One might assume only one version of a particular assembly can be registered with the global assembly cache at a time. Such a scenario, however, would defeat the capability of *side-by-side installation.* Side-by-side installation allows there to be more than one version of a component on the same machine. Instead, the global assembly cache enables the deployment of many different versions of the same file. You can verify this from a DOS prompt by listing all the files located within the assembly cache (**dir c:\winnt\assembly*.* /s**).

Because one assembly's manifest includes the version information of any additional assemblies referenced, the CLR loads the version specified in the manifest. In fact, if the major or minor versions of the referenced assembly are different than any stored in the GAC (or located in the application directory), the file won't load. Therefore, to apply a patch, be sure the version number matches the previous version and only the build and/or revision numbers change. Note, however, this isn't true for local assemblies in the same directory. Assemblies in the local directory or referenced in the configuration file are loaded regardless of the version number.

In summary, .NET component versioning is designed to solve many of the problems that previously existed on the Windows platform. Components shared by multiple applications are packaged into assemblies and deployed into the global assembly cache. Any application that references an assembly in the global cache looks for the specific version number it was built with, matching up both the major and minor parts of the version number. This enables the capability to deploy two or more versions of the same component on one machine and to be sure they reference the correct version.

If, however, multiple applications aren't sharing the component, then copying the file into the directory of the application is all that's required. For these scenarios, it's no longer necessary to register your component with the system. Installing applications by simply copying them on to the hard drive is often referred to as *xcopy deploy,* after the command line utility called **xcopy.exe**.

Built-in Metadata

Earlier in the chapter, we used **ILDasm.exe** to examine the assembly manifest to see what modules and external assemblies it referenced. Another key concept that can be viewed with **ILDasm.exe** is the inclusion of metadata into every data definition. As stated in Chapter 1, every data type within .NET software includes metadata that describes it. Furthermore, as you soon see when we look at reflection, all this metadata is accessible programmatically enabling developers to read and call into objects dynamically at runtime. Essentially, metadata is built into the IL.

NOTE

Through metadata, .NET software becomes self-describing.

With metadata, the CLR knows the layout of each object in memory. (The details of memory management appear later in this chapter.) This is important for the garbage collector when it comes to compacting the data. Without this knowledge, the garbage collector wouldn't know where one object instance ends and the next begins. Memory layout is also key when it comes to overflow checking. Because the CLR knows the size of all objects, it can prevent security breaches that involve overflowing a data area. Armed with metadata, the CLR can prevent code from accessing memory it shouldn't. Also, because the metadata is inherently part of IL code and IL code exists at runtime, little chance exists of any data-type mismatch occurring while code is executing, thereby increasing application reliability.

NOTE

Metadata in .NET enables the capability to check for overflow, thus sealing a potential security hole.

Metadata also aids in programming component software. Through the metadata, tools such as IntelliSense can operate even if the class is defined inside an entirely different module or assembly from the one you're writing. When you use editors that don't support IntelliSense, developers can examine metadata while programming against a particular class to view the exact definition of a class, even if no help file is supplied. In fact, a similar technique can be used to assist in generating documentation of your own classes.

If you continue on from programming to compiling and running your code, you'll realize metadata is used by the compilers, CLR, and debuggers. For example, metadata is used by the CLR to locate and load the modules that are part of an assembly, and then ensure that code executes within the bounds of the assigned security privileges.

Metadata defines a standard via which all programming languages can share a common format for interoperability. Rather than each language having its own custom mechanism for exposing type information, they can all use the common format of .NET metadata. Each compiler can use a standard format for exporting data type information. The same mechanism is used in the reverse. Rather than each language having a custom way of importing the metadata, each can use a common mechanism. For example, prior to .NET, C++ COM clients required the use of header files. In the most recent version, these could be generated using the **#import** precompile construct of Visual Studio 6. Visual Basic 6 didn't support the same mechanism, however, and header files were completely useless. Instead, Visual Basic required an oleautomation-compatible type library, which it then referenced. In the .NET world, the mechanism is significantly simpler: each language has the same mechanism in which the differences are syntactical, rather than methodological.

Metadata is absolutely essential to the JIT compiler. The JIT compiler can translate MSIL code into native machine code via metadata. Furthermore, through metadata, the CLR knows how to pass data from one context to another (*context* is the surrounding runtime environment, the walls or boundary, in which an object runs. The context is defined by such items as the security parameters, thread identity, and process characteristics within which an object is instantiated.) Metadata is a key ingredient to the CLR when it comes to data marshalling or passing data between contexts. In the COM world, writing custom marshalling code to handle anything but the most basic data types (known as *oleautomation data types*) was often necessary. Because of the intrinsic metadata that accompanies all managed data types, this is no longer necessary. Clearly, metadata is a core part of the .NET architecture.

Attribute-based Programming

As discussed in the previous chapter, the .NET framework provides several standard attributes and, in addition, you can create your own custom attributes. Custom attributes provide additional metadata that can be embedded into your class and examined at runtime via reflection code, which is written to interpret and respond to the attributes at runtime.

NOTE

Custom attributes don't affect the IL code a compiler generates.

NOTE

Custom attributes only become meaningful when code executing at runtime examines the metadata and looks for a particular attribute.

Consider an example. Imagine you wrote a set of classes that all fit within an application model. Furthermore, imagine for each type of class, you have a property that uniquely identifies the object. This property would serve as a primary key for all the objects of that type in the system. For example, if you have an object of type **Person**, you may assign the Social Security number as the primary key attribute because it uniquely identifies all the person objects. Since each object may have a different property that serves as the primary key, you decide to identify the field using a custom attribute.

To begin, you need to define the attribute. This is done by creating a new class that's derived from **System.Attribute**, as shown in the following example. (Note, all code for this section on attributes can be found in the file named **PKAttribute.cs**.)

```
namespace CSharpHeadStart
{
  [AttributeUsage(AttributeTargets.Class, AllowMultiple = false)]
  public class PrimaryKeyAttribute : System.Attribute
  {
    public PrimaryKeyAttribute(string Name)
    {
      this.Name = Name;
    }

    public string Name
    {
      get { return name; }
      set { name = value; }
    }

    private string name;
  }
}
```

In this example, we defined an attribute called **PrimaryKeyAttribute**, which can be used to decorate any class only once (**[AttributeUsage(AttributeTargets.Class, AllowMultiple = false)]**).

NOTE

*All the code within this section uses properties rather than fields because this provides an easier way to extend the functionality without changing the code in the **PrimaryKey** attribute.*

```
[PrimaryKey("SSN")]
public class Person : System.Object
{
  public Person(string SSN, string FirstName, string LastName)
  {
    this.SSN = SSN;
    this.FirstName = FirstName;
```

```
      this.LastName = LastName;
    }
    public string FirstName
    {
      get { return firstname; }
      set { firstname = value; }
    }
    public string LastName
    {
      get { return lastname; }
      set { lastname = value; }
    }
    public string SSN
    {
      get { return ssn; }
      set { ssn = value; }
    }

    private string firstname;
    private string lastname;
    private string ssn;
  }
```

Notice only one public constructor exists for this class and it takes a string. The result is if we use the attribute, as shown in the previous code, you must specify a string. For example, if the person attribute was decorated with [**PrimaryKey**] instead of [**PrimaryKey("SSN")**], the code wouldn't compile. Notice the name of the custom defined attribute is **PrimaryKeyAttribute**, but when it's actually used in the code, only **PrimaryKey** is used; the **Attribute** suffix is removed. The removal of the Attribute suffix isn't required, instead this is a characteristic of the C# compiler, and not an official part of the .NET specification. If you glance at the generated IL code, you'll notice the full name, including the suffix, is used. One last thing to note is the suffix Attribute is used by convention and isn't actually a requirement (although the convention should be followed).

Reflection

Now that we've seen how to create a custom attribute, it's time to look at accessing the attribute. The mechanism for doing this is known as *reflection* and it's much more generic than simply looking for a custom attribute. With reflection, you can read all the metadata of an assembly and its classes, and, from this, you could do things like generate code on the fly or automatically create documentation of your classes.

Although you can place the code for retrieving the custom attribute into a new class, for this example, the best place to add the code is into static functions on the **PrimaryKeyAttribute**. To begin, the following code shows a **GetPrimaryKeyName( )** function that should be added to the **PrimaryKeyAttribute** class.

```
public static string GetPrimaryKeyName(Type PKObjecType)
{
  // Now lets do some reflection
  Object[] pkattributes =
    PKObjecType.GetCustomAttributes(typeof(PrimaryKeyAttribute));
  if(pkattributes.Length > 0)
  {
    PrimaryKeyAttribute PKAttribute =
      (PrimaryKeyAttribute)pkattributes[0];
    return PKAttribute.Name;
  }
  else
    return null;
}
```

The function takes an object type (a class) as a parameter and retrieves the custom attributes of this type. **System.Type** is at the core of most of the reflection services and because **System.Object** supports this property, all objects provide the capability to retrieve it. Once the **PrimaryKeyAttribute** object has been retrieved, you can call the **Name** property to retrieve the name of the primary field property.

The following code demonstrates how to use the **GetPrimaryKeyName( )** function. It begins by opening an assembly and searching through each module's classes. Given each class, it checks for the **PrimaryKeyAttribute** and, if this exists, it prints the name of the property specified.

```
namespace CSharpHeadStart
{
  class EntryPoint
  {
    static public void Main()
    {
      string PKName;
      Assembly assembly = Assembly.Load("Person.dll");
      foreach (Module module in assembly.GetModules())
        foreach (Type type in module.GetTypes())
```

```
            {
               PKName = PrimaryKeyAttribute.GetPrimaryKeyName(type);
               if( PKName != null )
                  Console.WriteLine(
                     "The primary key of class '{0}' is '{1}'",
                     type.ToString(), PKName );
               else
                  Console.WriteLine("Class '{0}' has no primary key.",
                     type.ToString());
            };
      }
   }
}
```

As already stated, reflection provides more than simply a documentation mechanism. Reflection can also be used to call functions dynamically. Look at the following code, for example, which is a listing of the entire **PrimaryKeyAttribute** class with a new static **GetPKValue( )** function included.

```
namespace CSharpHeadStart
{
   [AttributeUsage(AttributeTargets.Class, AllowMultiple = false)]
   public class PrimaryKeyAttribute : System.Attribute
   {
      public PrimaryKeyAttribute(string Name)
      {
         this.Name = Name;
      }

      public string Name
      {
         get { return name; }
         set { name = value; }
      }

      private string name;

      // This method returns the name of the primary key
      // field given an object. Null is returned if the
      // object has no properties with the PrimaryKey
      // attribute
      public static string GetPrimaryKeyName(Type PKObjecType)
```

```
  {
    // Now lets do some reflection
    Object[] pkattributes =
      PKObjecType.GetCustomAttributes(typeof(PrimaryKeyAttribute));
    if(pkattributes.Length > 0)
    {
      PrimaryKeyAttribute PKAttribute =
        (PrimaryKeyAttribute)pkattributes[0];
      return PKAttribute.Name;
    }
    else
      return null;
  }


// This function returns the value of the property
// identified as the primary key or null if no
// such field exists.
public static object GetPKValue(Object PKObject)
{
    System.Reflection.PropertyInfo propertyInfo = null;
    string primaryKeyName =
      PrimaryKeyAttribute.GetPrimaryKeyName(PKObject.GetType());
    if(primaryKeyName != null)
    {
      propertyInfo = PKObject.GetType().GetProperty(
        primaryKeyName);
    }

    if(propertyInfo!= null)
    {
      return propertyInfo.GetValue(PKObject, null).ToString();
    }
    else
    {
      // The attribute must have been on a field or method
      // which are not covered here or else no PK attribute
      // was specified.
      return null;
    }
  }
}
}
```

The added **GetPKValue( )** function is designed to take an object as a parameter and return the value stored in this object's primary key property. Given this object, the function first calls **GetPrimaryKeyName( )** to retrieve the name of the property decorated with the **PrimaryKeyAttribute** attribute. Next, it uses the type of the object parameter—**PKObject**—and requests a **System.Reflection.PropertyInfo** object. The **PropertyInfo** object is then used to retrieve the value stored in the class property identified by the **PrimaryKeyAttribute**.

In the previous code, **PropertyInfo** was used because the attribute was intended to identify the primary key property. This isn't enforced at compile time, however, and developers could specify a method or a field when using the **PrimaryKeyAttribute**. To account for this scenario, you would have to use the **FieldInfo** or **MethodInfo** class. (This isn't shown in the previous listing because it makes the listing too long, but it's reasonably trivial to add it.) All of these derive from **MemberInfo** and offer similar functionality.

The following code demonstrates how to call the **GetPKValue( )** function.

```
namespace CSharpHeadStart
{
  class EntryPoint
  {
    static public void Main()
    {
      // Instantiate a person
      Person person = new Person(
        "781-00-7865", "Abraham", "Lincoln");

      string PKName = PrimaryKeyAttribute.GetPrimaryKeyName(
        person.GetType());

      // Now lets retrieve the name of the primary key property.
      Console.WriteLine("The primary key of class {0} is {1}",
        person.GetType(), PKName);

      // Now let's dynamically execute some code and retrieve
      // the value of the property.
      Console.WriteLine("The value of the '{0}' property " +
        "on class '{1}' is '{2}'.",
        PKName, person.GetType().ToString(),
        PrimaryKeyAttribute.GetPKValue( person ).ToString());
    }
  }
}
```

In this code, we begin by instantiating a **Person** object. Next, we retrieve the primary key name from the type of the instantiated object—in this case, **Person**—and write this out to the console. Finally, we call the **GetPKValue( )** function to retrieve the function value. In this case, the result would be "781-00-7865."

Cross-language Interoperability

One of the key features MSIL enables is *cross-language interoperability,* which allows developers to write code in multiple .NET languages and to have it all interact as though it were written in the same language (which it is because each language compiles into IL).

Take, for example, the following Visual Basic.NET code.

```
Namespace CSharpHeadStart

  Class VBBase
    Public Overridable Function Identify() As String
        Return "VBBase"
    End Function
  End Class

End Namespace
```

Given this class, you can create a C# class that derives from the **VBBase** class, as the following demonstrates.

```
namespace CSharpHeadStart
{
  class CSharpDerived : VBBase
  {
    public new string Identify()
    {
      return "CSharpDerived";
    }
  }
  class EntryPoint
  {
    public static void Main()
    {
```

```
CSharpDerived cs =  new CSharpDerived();
VBBase vb = new VBBase();
System.Console.WriteLine(cs.Identify());
System.Console.WriteLine(vb.Identify());
vb = cs;
// CSharpDerived output since Identify()
// is virtual in VBBase.
System.Console.WriteLine(vb.Identify());      }
   }
}
```

Simply including the Visual Basic module (using the **/addmodule** option) when compiling your C# code is the only additional step to achieving language interoperability. Note, language interoperability doesn't enable you to include two different languages within the same file or even to compile two files of different languages into the same module. Each language needs to be compiled into its own module or assembly before interoperability can work.

Exception handling can even be used across languages. In other words, you can throw an exception from one language and catch it using code written in a different language. This type of functionality wasn't supported at all before and COM developers were required to take great care in ensuring that C++ exceptions were never thrown across COM boundaries. With .NET, however, cross boundary exception handling becomes a concern of the past.

Another significant feature of language interoperability is cross-language debugging. In fact, debugging not only crosses language boundaries, it can also cross process and machine boundaries, displaying code regardless of what language it's written in.

Common Language Specification

To ensure components have language interoperability, Microsoft has defined a standard called the Common Language Specification (CLS). Because of syntactical characteristics in various languages, CLS places some additional restrictions on code so that it will be fully interoperable with other languages. The most relevant of these restrictions for C# programmers concerns case sensitivity. Some languages, such as Visual Basic, aren't case-sensitive. The result is this: if you define a class in C# with two functions that only differ in case, then this function won't be interoperable with all .NET languages. This is because case-insensitive languages cannot distinguish between the two methods. This restriction is placed on all public and protected members of a class. Another restriction is that overloaded operators should have alternate-named functions that perform the same operation because not all languages allow operator overloading. Other criteria must be met for a class to be CLS-compliant. The details can be found in the CLS documentation. Despite the CLS restrictions, language interoperability is well ahead of previous solutions to this problem. Previously, for languages to interoperate, each language's compiler had to generate assembler code that conformed to a binary standard, and the final restrictions were much greater.

To write CLS-compliant C# code (something that's recommended if you plan on distributing your components for others to use), you need to decorate it with the **CLSCompliant** attribute. The following is sample code demonstrating how to do this:

```
[assembly:System.CLSCompliant(true)]
namespace CSharpHeadStart
{
    class ThisClassIsCLSCompliant
    {
        . . .
    }
}
```

You can also check if an assembly is CLS-compliant using the **PEVerify.exe** tool.

Common Type System

Another aspect IL maintains control over is in the types available in the .NET Framework. As you saw in the last chapter, a fixed set of types is available with .NET: classes, interfaces, and value types. The type system plays an important role in cross-language integration because it defines the rules language compilers need to abide by for their code to interoperate with other languages. Because, ultimately, all language compilers will generate IL code, each language is forced to comply with the Common Type System if the language is a managed language. The Common Type System (CTS) describes the types supported by the .NET Framework and how these types interrelate to each other.

Object-oriented

Another key characteristic of IL is that it is object-oriented. In the previous chapter, you read about the object-oriented features offered by C#. In this section, you see how each of these features is really a C# way of exposing the same features found in IL. Performing this analysis serves two purposes: first, it provides a firsthand look at the intimate role the .NET Framework plays in the language of C#; and, second, it provides a cursory look at the IL language. Becoming familiar with IL code is valuable simply because IL is such an integral part of .NET. Let's look at some of the code you previously saw in C# and examine the resulting IL code.

To begin, remember all classes are ultimately derived from **System.Object**, whether they're explicitly coded as such and regardless of what managed language they're written in. The following **SimpleProgram** class (taken from Chapter 2's **Hello.cs**), therefore, is derived from **System.Object**.

```
class SimpleProgram
{
  ...
}
```

To see this, look at the following compiled IL code:

```
.class auto ansi SimpleProgram extends ['mscorlib']System.Object
{
} // end of class 'SimpleProgram'
```

As you open and view more and more classes in .NET, you find they're all derived from **System.Object**. Even value type objects have their roots in **System.Object**. (**System.Object** itself, along with interfaces are the exceptions.)

Another interesting feature of the **Hello.exe** IL code is the explicit inclusion of **mscorlib**. **Mscorlib** is the assembly that contains the **System.Object** class. The square brackets around a module name like this indicate the module in which the following class is located. Part of the IL code for interoperability between classes in different modules, therefore, is to identify where a particular class or data type is defined.

One final item to notice in the previous code is the **extends** keyword, which is used to designate an inheritance relationship. Therefore, if, instead of deriving from **System.Object**, **SimpleProgram** is derived from **CSharpHeadStartProgram**, the resulting IL code would be as follows:

```
.class private auto ansi SimpleProgram
       extends CSharpHeadStartProgram
{
} // end of class SimpleProgram
```

Curiously, the keyword for interface inheritance isn't the same as for class inheritance. Instead of using the keyword **extends**, interface inheritance uses **implements**. Therefore, the following C# code (taken from **Interface1.cs**)

```
interface IEmployee
{
  ...
}
...
class Doctor : IEmployee
{
  ...
}
```

results in IL code that looks like this:

```
.class private auto ansi Doctor
       extends [mscorlib]System.Object
       implements IEmployee
{
} // end of class Doctor
```

The **implements** keyword doesn't replace the **extends** keyword. As you can see, **Doctor** is still derived from **System.Object**. However, in addition, all the methods of **IEmployee** result in implementations on the **Doctor** class. In C#, whenever you specify an inheritance relationship to an interface, the C# compiler generates IL code that uses the **implements** keyword.

NOTE

*IL code uses the **implements** keyword to identify inheritance from interfaces.*

This is consistent with the multiple inheritance rules found in C#. A class must have one and only one other class from which it derives; it can **extend** exactly one class. In contrast, multiple inheritance is supported for interfaces. Therefore, the C# compiler can generate a class or value type that **implements** any number of interfaces.

Delegation and Events

Delegation and events are also features inherently supported in C# because they are .NET/IL features. Let's look at the IL code generated from the **delegates.cs** file discussed in Chapter 2. In this code, a delegate called **CallEmployeeDelegate** was declared as follows:

```
delegate void CallEmployeeDelegate();
```

If you open up a compiled assembly with **ILDasm.exe**, however, you see the C# compiler generates a new class using this declaration and this class is derived from **System.MulticastDelegate**.

```
.class private auto ansi sealed CallEmployeeDelegate
       extends [mscorlib]System.MulticastDelegate
{
} // end of class SimpleDelegate
```

This demonstrates the implementation of delegation within .NET is actually a continuation of the object-oriented nature of the IL language. Once you understand **CallEmployeeDelegate** is actually a class derived from **System.MulticastDelegate**, and it includes a constructor and various methods, it becomes easy to realize the invocation involved in calling a delegate is simply a reinterpretation of any method call on an object.

In this case, the C# design team decided it was more useful for developers if C# obfuscated the underlying architecture of delegation and, instead, included the keyword **delegate** as a means for automatically declaring delegates.

Memory Management Through Garbage Collection

Probably one of the most appealing aspects of .NET programming, at least for C++ programmers, is that memory management no longer needs to be of such primary importance when coding. Such practices as paring up **new** with **delete**, **AddRef( )** with **Release( )**, and **malloc( )** with **free( )** are relegated to the way of punch cards when programming in the managed world. The reason is all objects in the .NET world are automatically garbage-collected by the CLR. When declaring a variable and allocating memory in the managed world, programmers no longer need be concerned with cleaning up the memory before the variable goes out of scope. Instead, the common language runtime takes responsibility for doing this. The result? A major programming headache for today's programmers will virtually disappear in .NET.

One of the most important characteristics of .NET garbage collection is this: although you can guarantee all managed objects will be freed, you cannot be sure when this deallocation will occur. Programmers need to shift from the mindset that once a reference variable goes out of scope, its memory will be immediately restored to the system. Just because an area of memory no longer has any references to it, doesn't mean the memory will be immediately released. All you can be sure of is it will be released.

In fact, in the .NET world, all objects (except the Value Types) are created on the *managed heap*. The heap is considered managed because whatever is allocated on the heap is under the control of the CLR garbage-collection facilities. In other words, although the managed heap bears some resemblance to the C runtime heap, you never have to free the objects explicitly. When a .NET application begins, the CLR reserves a portion of memory for data that the application may need. As objects are created, the portion of reserved area the object requires is then initialized to the initial state of the object. The heap then moves a next-object pointer to the area immediately following the newly allocated object, so it knows where to place the next requested object.

Before an object can be created, the CLR first checks to see if enough remaining space is in the reserved area. If this isn't the case, however, then the garbage collector is run to try to free up allocated memory that is no longer being used but still allocated. Although the garbage collector can be programmatically triggered to run, in general, it only runs when the managed heap no longer has enough room for a new object or because the application is being terminated. The result is that object deallocation occurs at an indeterminate time after the object is no longer referenced. For many C++ programmers, this is a significant drawback with few workarounds, but we'll postpone a discussion of possible workarounds until Chapter 5. Meanwhile, let's look at a few more of the details in the garbage-collection algorithm.

Garbage Collection Step-by-Step

The first step in running the garbage collector is probably the most shocking to performance addicts. Although the garbage collector runs on a different thread than your application, this doesn't mean your application threads can continue to run as the garbage-collection algorithm executes. Unfortunately, because the garbage collector actually moves objects in the reserved area, suspending all managed threads from executing is necessary, so all pointers to moved objects can be updated to point to the new location. (While creating special threads that aren't interrupted is possible, this is beyond the scope of this introduction.) Details of this are described shortly, but readers need to be aware of this interruption in execution. Although the entire garbage collection process is fast, it isn't concurrent with your program's execution. Now, lets look at how it works.

To begin, we consider the two blocks or tables shown in Figure 3-2. The right block is the previously introduced reserved area. In the left block, *root objects*, which mark the beginning of object-dependency trees that run through an

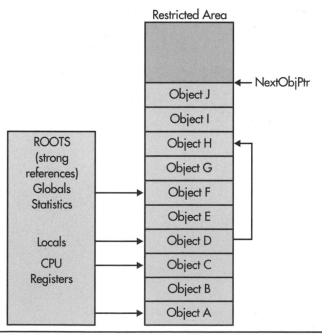

Figure 3-2   *The root objects referencing objects in the managed heap.*

application, are placed. These objects are held in memory because they're usually explicitly declared inside your application. The following is a list of possible root objects:

▶ global and static object pointers

▶ reference type local variables on the stack

▶ function call parameters on the stack

▶ CPU registers pointing to objects on the heap

▶ freachable pointers (to be defined later)

Most notably missing from the list are instance-member variables. A list of each of these root objects is kept by the CLR and, when the garbage collector runs, it traverses this list to identify all objects referenced in the reserved area. In the process of traversing the dependency tree, the garbage collector marks those objects it encounters. This reduces the amount of processing required by not retraversing objects and preventing the infinite loop case where two or more objects refer to each other.

Once all the roots are traversed, the garbage collector can walk the heap and compact it by moving the remaining referenced objects together. As it does this, the garbage collector also marks the various sections in the heap, based on an object's generation. Objects that have been through two or more garbage collection cycles are located in Generation 2 (no generations go beyond Generation 2 at this time). Objects that have only encountered one garbage collection cycle are in Generation 1. As objects get created, they're all placed into Generation 0, until the garbage collector runs and they're either de-allocated or compacted into the next generational area. Figure 3-3 shows the heap as it goes through a garbage collector cycle. In this diagram, the arrows from the root block are arbitrarily added and removed to simulate changes.

The last step in the process is to update each pointer, so it points to an object's new location. This involves updating not only all roots, but also pointers inside objects on the heap that point to other objects on the heap. As stated at the beginning of this section, it is this step that requires all managed threads to be paused while the garbage collector runs.

The advantage of segregating the managed heap into generations is that it enables various optimizations to be performed. For example, rather than the garbage collector compacting the entire heap, it could restrict its activity to Generation 0. This can significantly help performance because fewer pointers need to be updated due to objects being moved. Some complexities exist when objects in Generations 1

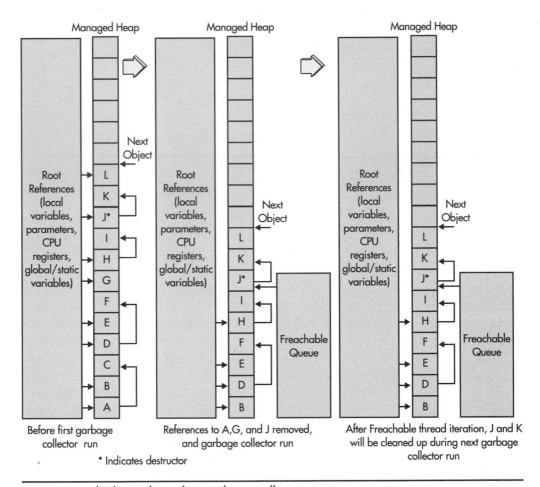

Figure 3-3   *The heap through a garbage collector*

or 2 create objects because the new objects are automatically placed in Generation 0, but means of tracking such activity exist. The key to generational garbage collection is this general performance assumption: the newer the object, the shorter its lifetime will be, and the older an object, the longer its lifetime will be.

Finalization

There is one more important process within the garbage collection cycle and it is known as *finalization*. Because *deterministic destruction* of objects doesn't exist—in other words, you cannot predict when an object will be cleaned up and the memory deallocated—IL code doesn't include the concept of a destructor. Although the .NET development languages may have such a concept, examination of IL code reveals destructors compile into a method called **Finalize( )**. Take, for example, the following short C# class:

```
class Destroyer
{
  ~Destroyer()
  {
      System.Console.WriteLine("Finalize called");
  }
}
```

If you examine this compiled code with **ILDasm.exe**, you see the resulting code looks like this:

```
.class private auto ansi Destroyer
  extends [mscorlib]System.Object
{
  .method family hidebysig virtual instance void
     Finalize() il managed
  {
  // Code size        17 (0x11)
  .maxstack  8
  IL_0000:  ldstr      "Finalize called"
  IL_0005:  call       void [mscorlib]System.Console::WriteLine(
    class System.String)
  IL_000a:  ldarg.0
  IL_000b:  call    instance void [mscorlib]System.Object::Finalize()
  IL_0010:  ret
  } // end of method Destroyer::Finalize

  .method public hidebysig specialname rtspecialname
     instance void .ctor() il managed
  {
  // Code size        7 (0x7)
  .maxstack  8
  IL_0000:  ldarg.0
  IL_0001:  call       instance void [mscorlib]System.Object::.ctor()
  IL_0006:  ret
```

```
    } // end of method Destroyer::.ctor

} // end of class Destroyer
```

The interesting item to note in this listing is that there is no destructor function, a **.dtor( )** corresponding to the **.ctor( )** constructor, for example. Instead, we have a new function called **Finalize( )**. The responsibility for calling the destructor (or **Finalize( )** method) is assigned to the garbage collector, so an additional step needs to be inserted into the garbage-collection algorithm. When the object is instantiated, the CLR detects that it contains a destructor and, in response, adds a reference to the object into a finalization queue. Surprisingly, this additional reference doesn't prevent the garbage collector from cleaning up the object, at least not directly. As the garbage collector executes, it determines one of these special objects needs to be cleaned up, just as it does normally. During the compacting routine, however, it checks the finalization queue to see if it contains a reference to the current object. If it does, then the object is placed into another queue called the *freachable queue.* Pointers in the freachable queue are considered roots and prevent the object from being cleaned up. The result is, even if the garbage collector continues though several more iterations, objects pointed to by only freachable pointers are still not cleaned up. So, how do these objects get reclaimed? The garbage collector includes a separate thread that iterates through the freachable queue and calls the destructors. Once this step is completed, the object is removed from the freachable queue, so it can finally be cleaned up when the garbage collector next runs.

NOTE

Exactly when the destructor will be called, after all references to an object are removed, is unknown.

Although the previous description is an oversimplified version of what takes place, readers should consider carefully whether they need a destructor. First, although a destructor is conceptually similar to the traditional destructor (such as those found in C++ and Visual Basic 6.0), when the method will get called after the object goes out of scope is unknown. Second, finalizable objects (those with destructors) require multiple iterations of the garbage collector to be deallocated, resulting in higher resource utilization over all. The impact of this is compounded by the fact that finalizable objects may refer to other nonfinalizable objects and also prevent these objects from being cleaned up. Because finalizable objects aren't added to the freachable queue in any particular order, the calls to an object's destructor won't be ordered either. This can cause some unpredictable results when destructors refer to contained objects. Given these caveats, developers should consider carefully whether to include a destructor in their class.

A full discussion on various solutions to the unavailability of a deterministic destructor in .NET is in Chapter 5. The simplest method, however, is to include a Dispose function in place of the destructor. Such a method wouldn't necessarily be called automatically, but it would provide a mechanism for clients of your class to call resource clean up explicitly.

In general, the memory management method previously described is blisteringly fast at allocating memory and, assuming your application doesn't require the garbage collector to run, there's relatively little cost for this performance enhancement. Even when the garbage collector does run, however, the algorithm is reasonably efficient and you can be sure it'll constantly be tweaked through each version of the CLR. Based on initial estimates, garbage collection times appear to be in the 1 millisecond range on processors as slow as 200 MHz. One last point to mention is two versions of the garbage collector exist: one is optimized for the single processor and one is optimized for multiprocessor machines.

Strong and Weak References

In the previous section, an object preventing the garbage collector from cleaning up another object on the heap is called a *strong reference.* All root objects, for example, are strong references because they're pointing to other objects in the heap and preventing those objects from being released. There is another kind of reference, however, called a *weak reference.* A weak reference is a class (**WeakReference**) that points to another object on the heap, but the weak reference won't prevent the garbage collector from cleaning up the object it points to. Essentially, the weak reference provides a means to indicate to the garbage collector, "I may use this object again, but I don't need it at the moment. Therefore, if you need the memory, reclaim it." This is in contrast to a strong reference that says, "I'm pointing to this object, so you can't reclaim it." A weak reference essentially provides an object cache. If you re-request an object and it happens to be in the cache, you can gain a performance improvement. If the garbage collector ran during the time between the last use and rerequest, then the object would have to be reinstantiated.

NOTE

Weak references provide a type of cache system to reuse large objects.

One example where this may be used is with a search function. Imagine you have to search a large number of objects to see if they fulfill some criteria. (Large refers to the amount of memory consumed, which is generally where weak references are used.) Also imagine you haven't yet instantiated the collection of objects. To accomplish the search, you would instantiate the collection and check the criteria against each object in the collection. Once the search completes, the normal procedure—assuming no weak references exist—is to allow the collection to go out of scope or be set to null, thereby freeing up the garbage collector to reclaim the memory. If the search needs to be repeated, possibly with different criteria, you would be required to reinstantiate the collection (and each object in the collection) because you no longer have a reference to it. If you never let the collection go out of scope, maintaining a reference to it, then the garbage collector could never reclaim the memory of the collection and all the objects within the collection. Contrast this with the use of a weak reference. Once the search completed the first time, you would instantiate a weak reference object as follows:

```
wkCollection = new WeakReference(collection);
```

Now, you would release the collection by assigning it to null. If, after some period of time, the collection is re-requested, then you would retrieve it from the **wkCollection** object after checking that the garbage collector hadn't reclaimed it. Here is the code:

```
collection = wkCollection.Target;
if (collection == null)
{
  // GC ran so re-instantiate the collection
  // and assign it to the collection variable.
}

// Now search collection
```

Note, any objects within the collection after the first search would also be cleaned up by the garbage collector if the collection only had a weak reference. However, any objects found during the search would have strong references (assuming they were now being used), so even if the collection were to be reclaimed, the found object would not.

Thread Synchronization

Developers are responsible for providing any necessary synchronization to the .NET classes because the vast majority of .NET classes are not thread-safe. This is because obtaining locks is a relatively expensive operation, which can lead to deadlocks without careful programming and degrade performance unnecessarily when no synchronization is required. The general methodology, therefore, is that you're responsible for providing all synchronization to an object when multiple threads can simultaneously access it.

Rather than creating entirely thread-safe classes, it's better to reduce the need for synchronization by designing your application so you limit the sharing of objects across multiple threads. Objects that aren't shared across multiple threads don't require any instance data synchronization. Therefore, assuming you're successful in not sharing objects across threads, you only need to be concerned with static data. The obvious solution to synchronization on static data is to avoid it having any static data. In cases where this isn't possible, however, an abundance of synchronization classes are provided by the .NET Framework.

The synchronization classes you can use within your application are **Interlocked, Monitor**, **ReaderWriterLock**, **ManualResetEvent**, and **AutoResetEvent**. Of these, **Monitor** has special support in C# because it can be used automatically by the **lock** keyword.

In C#, the **lock** keyword provides a mechanism for code block synchronization, so you needn't manually place a **try-catch-finally** block around the **Monitor** class-locking mechanism to be sure to release the lock. Instead, C# does this for you automatically via the **lock** keyword. The following code demonstrates how to use **lock**:

```
lock (typeof(MyClass))
{
  // Place synchronized block here
}
```

In this case, **typeof(<class>)** is specified as what to lock on. In other words, the lock is identified by the **typeof(<class>),** so if a different thread encounters an existing lock on the same class elsewhere, the code is blocked. Use **typeof(<class>)** to synchronize static data. If you need to synchronize instance data (meaning you were required to share the object across multiple threads), use **this** as the reference type on which to lock on. The lock keyword effectively expands to the following C# code:

```
System.Threading.Monitor.Enter(typeof(MyClass));
try {
```

```
      // Synchronized block will be here
}
finally {
   System.Threading.Monitor.Exit(typeof(MyClass));
}
```

If you're using synchronization to increment or decrement a variable, then you can use the static methods on the **Interlocked** class instead. For example, the following code demonstrates how to increment a shared variable:

```
protected static int instanceCount;
System.Threading.Interlocked.Increment(instanceCount);
```

In addition to increment and decrement methods, the **Interlocked** class also provides **Exchange( )** and **CompareExchange( )** methods for replacing the data in a variable.

If you are going to be distributing your classes to third parties, you should design them to run under multi-threaded server conditions because of the prevalence of Internet based applications and Application Service Providers (ASPs). The general design guideline for running on the server is the same as what was previously described. In other words, provide synchronization for all static data. You needn't synchronize instance data, however, because it's better to design the server application so that objects aren't shared across requests (threads). If you are unable to avoid sharing objects across requests, then you're responsible for synchronizing such objects.

C# Language Comparisons

IN THIS CHAPTER:

Comparing C# to C++

Comparing C# to Visual Basic.Net

Comparing C# to Java

In this section, we compare C# to C++, Visual Basic.NET, and Java. The information contained in this chapter is provided so you know which language to use when, not to advocate one language over another. .NET largely neutralizes most of the differences among the .NET languages. The functional differences come about as a result either of decisions that language designers made in exposing the underlying .NET features and functions or, in the case of C++, because of its legacy. The remaining differences are then simply a matter of syntax. The bottom line in this is for "pure" .NET applications, no reason exists for a significant functional difference between an application written in C#, Visual Basic.NET, or Managed Extensions for C++ (Managed C++).

Performance advantages of one language over another are also largely negated by .NET. The performance of managed applications should be nearly equal and, if they aren't, this is more than likely to be a bug in the language compiler, rather than a specific performance advantage of one language over another. This goes against current conventional thinking when it comes to Visual Basic versus C++. Previous to .NET, when a programmer needed maximum speed, C++ was the only choice (if assembler is counted, that would be two choices). Conversely, when a programmer needed to deliver something in the shortest amount of time, Visual Basic was often used or at least was a viable option.

This sets the stage for what is about to come—individual comparisons of C# to C++, Visual Basic.NET, and Java.

Comparing C# to C++

In this section, we compare C++ with C#. We don't cover all the differences but, instead, we focus on particular ones that argue for one language being preferable over another. As stated at the beginning of this book, C# was designed as the language of choice for C++ programmers who wanted to write managed code. Given this heritage, it's no surprise that C# shares significant syntax with C++. Despite the similarities, however, a number of differences exist. To begin our comparison of C# with C++, we focus mostly on syntactical differences. The differences are relatively minor and, in most cases, the C# development team introduced them to reduce the common pitfalls that occurred in C++. As we delve further into the discussion, we begin to look at the language differences from a higher level, examining some structural and compilational differences, as well as object-oriented differences. We end with some of the more significant differences that may warrant choosing one language over another for a particular purpose.

Before we begin any of this, however, we need to define what is meant by C++. In other words, as we compare C++ to C#, we need to be aware of which C++ version we're comparing C# to. We have C++ the language, C++ the development platform—including libraries such as the MFC library and ATL—and, lastly, C++ the development environment, which, for our purposes, is Visual Studio for C++. As if this isn't enough, .NET also introduces Managed Extensions for C++, which extends C++ into the managed environment.

.NET provides Managed Extensions for C++ to support the development of managed .NET applications in C++. Aside from the syntactical C++ difference, which we begin considering shortly, writing code in Managed C++ is functionally equivalent to writing C# code. Despite this, developers would be ill-advised to believe that managed C++ and C# are essentially identical. For example, the Visual Studio 7 Win Forms Designer only supports writing C# or Visual Basic code, not C++ (managed or unmanaged).

The majority of other differences between Managed C++ and C# are essentially syntactical, but the syntax weighs in C#'s favor. Unlike Visual Basic, which was able to undergo a radical transition because no cross-vendor standards existed, Managed C++ was forced to fit in with the well-established C++ language specification. This is essentially a good thing, except Managed C++ was still left without many of the syntactical improvements C# made to its predecessor. The bottom line is this: writing components in Managed C++ is harder than C#. Just the special syntax of managed extensions alone should cause people to think twice about doing C++ component development (never mind all the C++ language pitfalls the C# designers could avoid because they were starting a new language).

In other words, it isn't likely programmers will write completely new applications in Managed C++. Rather, it is expected that programmers will write some portions of a program in Managed C++ and the rest will remain in pre-existing MFC/ATL C++. The use of MFC/ATL, combined with Managed C++, assumes a large base of C++ code that was written prior to the .NET framework. Alternatively, Managed C++ may simply provide access to specific features of C++ that aren't supported by C# and .NET (templates, for example).

For the rest of this section on comparing C++ to C#, we focus on describing differences between C# and the nonmanaged form of C++, even though many of the differences do apply to both Managed C++ and native C++. Chapter 6 includes a relatively detailed discussion on integrating existing C++ code using the Managed Extensions for C++ into your .NET application.

Declarative Order Insignificant

The first syntactical difference between the two languages under consideration here is that C# doesn't enforce forward declarations. In other words, programmers needn't be concerned with making sure a particular data structure is declared earlier in the source code, before it was actually used. The C++ requirement of always defining data structures prior to their use forces developers to accommodate the way the compiler works, rather than the structure that best suits the program being written. In some ways, forcing an order to the way classes are declared subtly implies a procedural, rather than an object-based approach to development. This isn't surprising given C++'s heritage in C.

The side effect of this rule for C# programmers is that variable scope rules in C# are more restrictive. In C#, duplicating the same name within a routine is illegal, even if it's in a separate code block. The following code won't compile in C#, for example, where as it's allowable in C++:

```
for(int i=0; i<input.Length; i++)
{
  char c = input[i];
  if(c==' ')
  {
    // ...
    break;
  }
}

char c;
```

The resulting error is "error CS0136: A local variable named 'c' cannot be declared in this scope because it would give a different meaning to 'c', which is already used in a 'child' scope to denote something else."

Assignment and Equality Operators Restricted

Another essentially syntactical difference relates to conditional expressions inside **if**, **which**, and **do** statements. Nearly every C++ programmer (if not all) has introduced a bug into their code because they used the C++ assignment operator (=) rather than the equality operator (==). The typical error goes something like this:

```
int i, j;
...
// LOGIC ERROR:
if(j=i),
   cout << i << " equals " << j << endl;
else
   cout << i << " does not equal " << j << endl;
```

To prevent a similar pitfall from entering into the C# syntax, C# requires the only data type that can be used in a conditional expression is a **bool**. The result is that the following C# code won't even compile.

```
int i, j;
...
// ERROR: Cannot implicitly convert type 'int' to 'bool'
if (i=j)
   Console.WriteLine("{0} equals {1}", i, j);
else
   Console.WriteLine("{0} does not equal {1}",
     i, j);
```

Not to be outdone, however, you can intentionally perform the assignment during a conditional statement if you want by calling the **ToBoolean( )** function on the **integer** as follows:

```
if ((i=j).ToBoolean())
   Console.WriteLine("i is {0}", i);
else
   Console.WriteLine("i is zero");
```

In other words, if you still want the C++ way of performing two operations at once, then so be it.

The converse of the previous error would be to use the equality operator in place of the assignment. This isn't as common and, even so, this particular error generates a warning on most modern day C++ compilers, so the fact that C# also prevents it is trivial.

Note, the previous distinction is the result of a higher level principal in C#. C# syntax requires that execution statements must do work and conditional statements may not do work (unless intentionally and explicitly coded to do so as in the

ToBoolean( ) example). In contrast to C++, therefore, you cannot have statements that don't perform any function in C#. The following is an example:

```
bool b;
if(b)
  // ERROR: Only assignment, call, increment, decrement, and
  // new expressions can be used as a statement
  "I ain't doing no work";
```

No Fall Through switch

Another potential pitfall for C++ programmers is to forget to call **break** during a switch statement, as the following demonstrates:

```
cout << "The value entered for j was ";
switch(j)
{
case 1:
  cout << "one";
  break;
case 2:
  cout << "two";
  // break missing so falls through
case 3:
  cout << "three";
  // break missing so falls through
default:
  cout << "greater than three";
}
```

To prevent this error, C# only executes one case statement. At the end of the case statement, C# requires an explicit jump statement be coded (**break, goto, continue,** or **return**). The goto statement can be used to implement the fall through that C++ uses by default.

```
string favoriteLanguage;
...
switch(favoriteLanguage)
{
  case "C#":
  case "CSharp":
```

```
      Console.WriteLine("C# is music to my ears");
      break;
   case "VB":
   case "Visual Basic":
      Console.WriteLine("Dim is not so dull");
      break;
   case "C":
      Console.WriteLine("I ain't got no stinkin class");
      goto case "C++";
   case "C++":
      Console.WriteLine("-> shows the way to go");
      break;
   default:
      Console.WriteLine("We are not talking French and German here");
      break;
}
```

Rather ironically, the explicit jump statement at the end of each case statement was included in the language specifications, so the code was clear for C++ developers who might not realize no fall through was supported in C#.

Note, one significant improvement over C++ syntax is the availability of using strings within the switch statements expression. This eliminates the need to set up an array that maps strings to integer or character values.

Exception Processing

One relatively minor feature C# supports, that isn't found in native C++ (Managed C++ does include this feature), is the **finally** statement. This is used to write termination code guaranteed to be called on exit from a try-catch block, whether or not an exception was called. To achieve the same result in native C++ requires programmers to duplicate the code in two places. In C++, each catch block must be sure to call a **finally( )** type function or use a **goto** in order to jump to a finally block. Even with the extra code, there's also the subtle case of an exception occurring within a catch block, which requires even more special handling. In C#, the finally block is written once and it's guaranteed to be called.

Iteration Using foreach

The **foreach( )** statement in C# was borrowed from Visual Basic and doesn't exist in C++ at all. The keyword is used to iterate over any object that explicitly or implicitly supports the **IEnumberable** interface. (The object must be derived from **IEnumberable** or simply implement all the functions of **IEnumberable** without actually being derived from it.) In C++ (and Java), equivalent functionality requires the **for** loop. The advantage of **foreach,** however, is it automatically detects the boundaries of the collection being iterated over. Furthermore, the **foreach** statement syntax includes a built-in iterator for accessing the current item in the collection. Using a regular for loop is a suitable solution, but the ease of use provided by the **foreach** adds one notch into the C# quiver. This is undoubtedly true when iterating through COM collection from C++. Such an exercise, although uncomplicated, requires an inordinate amount of code in comparison to the **foreach** statement. It deserves mention that many of the STL collections do provide similar features as the **foreach** statement. However, STL iteration is still more complicated than **foreach**.

Additional Native Data Types

Because C++ doesn't support a native string type, all but the most basic of string manipulations require an additional library, such as the STL library. Even with the standard C runtime library, strings are second-class citizens because string manipulation functions are essentially procedural rather than object-oriented. For example, rather than calling an external function to convert a string to an integer as you would in C++, C# supports the **ToInt32( )** function as a member of the string class.

One class that diminishes the significance of not having a native string type is MFC's **CString**, which can now be included into your projects without having to link to MFC. Even so, C++ programmers won't mourn the loss of the **BSTR** data structure, which required careful thought when it came to memory management, even with the help of MFC's **CString,** ATL's **CComBSTR**, or Visual C++'s compiler COM support class **_bstr_t**.

Finally, C# programmers can disregard whether the string they're manipulating is a wide-character string or an ANSI string. This means you no longer need to surround all literal strings with and **_T** or an **_TEXT**. More importantly, because the .NET Framework is supported on all Windows 9*x* platforms and beyond, you no longer need to deliver both a multibyte and a UNICODE version of your binary files.

NOTE

C#, and the .NET framework in general, have virtually eliminated the inordinate amount of attention the strings required to write code for both UNICODE and multibyte character compile.

One last minor point regarding strings: C# provides the capability to enter string literals verbatim. For example, rather than prefixing every backslash character with an escape character (a second backslash), C# can interpret the string verbatim. This reduces the number of errors that occurred in C++ when quoting paths. The following is a C# verbatim string.

```
··string dangIt = @"Why can't the $%@#(?%\n%!@#$ compiler
····do what I mean and not what I tell it.";
··Console.Write("{0}", dangIt);
```

Note, the line-feed character is also interpreted literally, along with the spaces that precede the first letter on the second line. In other words, the output from this is as follows:

```
Why can't the $%@#(?%\n%!@#$ compiler
····do what I mean and not what I tell it.
```

In both listings, a '·' character represents a space at the beginning of the line.

NOTE

C#'s bool data type cannot be implicitly or explicitly cast to any data type except object.

In C#, Boolean is a native type and cannot be converted to any other type without explicitly calling a conversion function on the class. Conversions like the following, for example, won't compile in C#.

```
bool b = true;
int i = (int)b;
```

This is relevant because it prevents errors that result from assuming true to be a particular value. Testing an integer for a value of true required checking for not false (or not equal to zero). Such errors were more frequent when programming for COM because the Boolean data type in COM was **VARIANT_BOOL**, which used –1 for true (**VARIANT_TRUE**). The result is a comparison of a **VARIANT_BOOL** with a C++ **bool** type which often yielded incorrect results if not handled correctly. For example, a comparison of **VARIANT_TRUE** with **true** would yield **false**, even though logically they're intended to represent the same value. By preventing C#'s **bool** (**System.Boolean**) from being cast—either implicitly or explicitly—to any other data, type errors, like those previously mentioned, can be curtailed. (To force a **Boolean** to an integer value in C#, you can use the instance method, **System.Boolean.ToInt32( )** or its equivalent.)

Another data type distinction is that **null** in C# is a keyword because, in fact, **null** is considered an intrinsic value. The implications of this aren't particularly great but, in some instances, errors in C++ could be eliminated, especially when passing a pointer along and forgetting to dereference the pointer. Because **NULL** is represented by a 0 in C++, the potential exists for a subtle bug (one of the worst kinds) to occur.

From the previous examples, you can gather that the distinguishing characteristics of C++ when it came to native data types were to reduce the occurrence of bugs that commonly occurred in C++. This same theme permeates most, if not all, of the syntactical differences between C# and C++.

NOTE

Because C# structs are value types, creating a complex "fundamental" type is possible, something that couldn't be done with C++.

Another significant difference when it comes to data types is that a **struct** in C# is a value type, as pointed out in Chapter 2. The result is new "fundamental" data types can be created and added to the language. This is something that was never possible in C++. Not surprisingly, it could be argued that such a feature could be abused by defining structs that are too large and, thereby, create a performance bottleneck. However, the C# documentation clearly states what the intention of custom structs should be and even includes guidelines on maximum memory footprints.

No Pointers Per Se

Because we mentioned the "pointer" word in the last section, let's discuss it next. C# has no pointer operators at least in safe code and C++ does (->, *, and &), which is one of the defining differences between C++ and C#. In C++, programmers need to pay vigilant attention as to whether or not they're programming variables that are pointers. In fact, this distinction is so significant that C++ has adopted a naming convention in which all pointers are prefixed with a *p*. C++ compilers are usually smart enough to notify you when you have inadvertently treated a pointer as a value or vice versa. In contrast, however, C# doesn't even require you to be aware of what type you're working with, at least as far as syntax goes. Whether an object is passed as a reference or as a value type makes no difference to the syntax of either the caller or the callee. This doesn't mean programmers can completely ignore whether the data type is a value or a reference but, for the most part, the distinction becomes periphery. For the majority of cases, C# programmers only need be concerned with identifying a reference or value type when defining a new data structure, or when deciding how parameters will be passed to a function.

Because no pointers are in C#, obviously, no pointers to functions exist. However, the .NET Frameworks delegate type fulfills the need for function pointers and does it better than C++. In C#, for example, you can define multicast delegates, which requires significantly less code (and, therefore, less work) than would be required in C++ for similar functionality.

One last word about pointers: C++ includes a void** pointer, which enables programmers to pass around structures of an unknown type. This feature is often referred to as returning a *covariant* data type when returning from a function call. Although void** isn't supported in C#, every data type in C# is derived from System.Object, as we already pointed out. You can cast any data type to a System.Object, therefore, and pass that between functions to achieve the same effect as void**. And, furthermore, because System.Object supports the GetType( ) function, you can always identify what type an object is, which isn't something easily supported with void**. In fact, a cast to and from a void** almost always requires the use of reinterpret_cast, which entirely removes any type safety the C++ compiler could support either at compile time or at runtime. The result is that a misinterpretation of the type could result in some unpleasant errors.

Arrays

Unlike native arrays defined in C++, a *C# array* is actually a class, System.Array. The result is arrays have built-in functionality for such operations as sorting, searching, and reversing. Although not inherently the same in C++, the same functionality is available in C++'s STL classes. In fact, the STL array/collection classes have the added advantage of supporting a specific data type rather than a generic type, such as an object. This is done through the use of templates, discussed a little later in this chapter.

Another syntactical difference between C++ and C# occurs in the declaration of an array. In C++, the square brackets ("[ ]") are associated with the type, not with the variable. In C++, the code would be:

```
int quadruple[2];
```

whereas in C#, the code is:

```
int[2] quadruple;
```

The difference is minor and, although some would argue the C# version is more logical, opinion is probably divided based on personal preference and what a programmer is most accustomed to. What is more significant about array declaration differences is that C# supports special syntax to initialize arrays efficiently. This syntax was covered in-depth in the Language Overview.

One last distinction is this: arrays in C# are always reference types rather than value types, as they are in C++.

No Preprocessor

At this point, we begin to move away from mainly syntactical differences and begin to examine more substantial items. The first of these is that C# doesn't have a preprocessor. On the positive side, this means C# compiles will usually be significantly faster than those performed by C++.

Because no preprocessor exists, there's also no #including of files. This, combined with the fact that predeclarations in C# aren't required, enables C# to combine the class declaration with the class's implementation. Some may argue that separating out the declaration from the implementation is a feature. However, given that interfaces can be used to achieve abstraction like this, coupled with the fact that a class can be viewed in an assembly without also examining the implementation, means whatever is offered by separate files isn't lost in C#. What isn't present, however, is the burden C++ programmers generally face in always having to modify two files whenever a class's definition changed. Rather than requiring programmers to edit both a header file and an implementation file, just to make a slight alteration in function signature, C# combines both in the same file. Furthermore, developers are freed from the burden of searching for the right header file to include, and then verifying it's included in the right order.

So far, not having a preprocessor offers some advantages to C#, but the cost of not having a preprocessor is no macro support in C#. Two main advantages exist to having macros. The first advantage is macros can be used to reduce repetitious typing. Consider the following trace macro:

```
#define TRACE(Code) Console.WriteLine(#Code " = {0}", Code)
```

In this example, **Code** isn't limited only to being a variable. Instead, you could place code snippets within the macro as follows:

```
TRACE(2*Math.PI*r);
```

This would yield an output of:

```
2*Math.PI*r =  31.415926535897931
```

Many macros can and should be replaced with functions, as is demonstrated by the following example.

```
#define SQUARE(x) x*x
n = SQUARE(1++)
```

Here **x** is incremented twice, which is almost certainly not what a user of the **SQUARE** macro would expect without examining the code. Clearly, one of the problems with macros is sometimes they cause unintended consequences. Assuming a macro writer avoids these, however, and assuming the macro cannot be replaced with a function, as is the case with the previous **TRACE** example, C# simply doesn't have an equivalent feature.

One advantage often touted to prove macros are better than functions is that the macro performs faster because all code is placed inline, avoiding the overhead of calling a function (stack allocation, and so forth). In C++, functions can be defined with the **inline** keyword, which instructs the compiler to replace a function call with the code of the function body directly inside the caller, exactly as a macro would. Although C# doesn't support the **inline** keyword, Microsoft claims the compiler is smart enough to know when to inline code automatically so, in theory, macros don't offer a performance benefit. A few instances where inlining may occur include property get and set accessors, and when using sealed types.

Note, even though C# doesn't support a preprocessor, it still includes limited implementations of **#define**, **#elif**, **#else**, **#endif**, **#error**, **#if**, **#line**, **#undef**, and **#warning**. These aren't full feature equivalents to C++ (obviously, or what would be the point of the previous discussion?). **#define** can only be followed by an identifier, for example, and the identifier cannot be assigned a value, as in

```
// This is not valid in C#
#define TRACELEVEL 5
```

In Chapter 5, we examine ways to overcome the lack of macro support in C#.

Note that C# also supports an attribute called **ConditionalAttribute** (**Conditional**). The **Conditional** attribute provides a compile time switch for compiling a function to a "no op" based on whether a string symbol is defined or not. If the string is not defined then the function body is not included in the compiled code. The following example demonstrates how to use the **Conditional** attribute.

```
[System.Diagnostics.Conditional("DEBUG")]
public static void ConditionalMethod()
{
  // Do stuff here
}
```

In the preceding case, **DEBUG** is the symbol that needs to be defined in order for the **ConditionalMethod( )** to be included. Note that even if **DEBUG** is not defined, you do not need to remove any function calls to **ConditionalMethod( )**. The compiled code will still contain the declaration of the method. The content will be an IL **nop** instruction, however, as shown in the third to last line that follows.

```
.method public hidebysig static void ConditionalMethod() il managed
{
  .custom instance void
    [mscorlib]System.Diagnostics.ConditionalAttribute::.ctor(
    class System.String) = ( 01 00 05 44 45 42 55 47 00 00 )
    // . ..DEBUG..
  // Code size       2 (0x2)
  .maxstack  8
  IL_0000:  nop
  IL_0001:  ret
} // end of method EntryPoint::ConditionalMethod
```

No Templates

Templates are a form of macro on steroids. Modern day C++ compilers include support for templates, and one solution C++ programmers might attempt in place of a macro in C# is to use templates. Unfortunately, this wouldn't be possible because C# doesn't support templates either. Templates, also known as *generics,* enable you to write a class or method generically for any type while maintaining the type identity. The data type is required to support any functions the template calls. The most common use of templates is for collection/container classes or (as with ATL) smart pointers, but other uses also exist.

Consider the following class:

```
struct point
{
  public point(
    double x, double y)
  {
    this.x = x;
    this.y = y;
  }
  public double x;
  public double y;
}
```

The class is clearly designed to handle a pair of coordinates. However, essentially nothing is unique about this class except that it contains two objects of a particular type, **Double**. What if you could define such a class that could generically contain any object? Such a class would require the use of templates, as follows:

```
template <class T, class U>
struct Pair
{
  public Pair(T First, U Second)
  {
    this.First - First;
    this.Second = Second;
  }
  public T First;
  public U Second;
}
```

This class can pair any two data types together even if they aren't the same. Essentially, a template enables you to write a class in which the type of data in the class is a parameter to the class at declaration time.

Unfortunately, C# doesn't support templates (at least not in Version 1.0) and no equivalent exists either. Chapter 5 includes a discussion of how to overcome this missing feature.

Multiple Inheritance

As you learned in the previous chapter, C# doesn't support multiple inheritance of classes, in contrast to C++, which does support them. The degree to which this is a problem is discussed at length in Chapter 5, along with some design decisions that can be made to reduce the need for multiple-inheritance. The bottom line, however, is that such a feature isn't supported. Some language purists argue this is a good thing because often the feature is misused. However, the world clearly has hierarchical relationships in which one object has *is-a* relationships with at least two other objects and, therefore, losing the entire structure to protect a few unsuspecting developers from making a poor design choice seems a pity.

Perhaps surprisingly for some, the story on multiple inheritance doesn't stop here, however. At the COM interface level in C++, multiple inheritance isn't supported either, whereas it is supported in C#. Interfaces in the C++ COM world are defined in a language known as interface definition language (IDL), although IDL doesn't let you define new interfaces derived from multiple interfaces.

Interfaces defined in IDL are used to generate C++ header files by the MIDL compiler and these header files use structs to declare the interface. C++ structs, however, do support multiple-inheritance, so why the restriction? Why can't the MIDL compiler simply combine the two interfaces into one, stacking them on top of each other in the vtable layout? The reason is that the exact vtable layout for an interface is immutable and, given that every interface must begin with the methods of **IUnkown** at its root, it isn't possible to lay one interface after another without duplicating the **IUnknown** methods or mutating the interface. Because the .NET Framework doesn't have the burden of supporting **IUnknown**, the abandonment of multiple interface inheritance isn't required, and is, instead, fully supported.

Calling Libraries

While we're discussing C# simply falling short of C++, let's examine calling external native libraries, more specifically, the Win32 API. C++ provides native access to Win32 system calls, as well as other third-party libraries. Included in standard C++ header files is a myriad of function declarations that make calling these APIs relatively trivial.

Not to be outdone, C# does provide a facility for making native Win32 calls, although this is slightly more difficult than C++ because it requires the programmer to declare the function by hand using an **import** statement. This can sometimes be a challenge for developers who aren't already familiar with the particular API being called or who simply don't have the Win32 experience to make the calls in the first place, regardless of the language. C# doesn't stop there, however. The vast library of classes included with the .NET Framework is intended to provide an object-oriented wrapper for the majority of the Win32 API set. This significantly reduces the need even to make direct Win32 calls and, instead, provides a vastly simpler object-oriented mechanism for making the calls.

Building Component Libraries

Without taking into account Managed C++, C++ basically offers two approaches for building and distributing components on the Windows platform. You can build a library DLL or build a COM server. Both require significantly more effort than C# and .NET.

Library DLLs require C style declarations and are generally only designed to interoperate with other C libraries (though, these days, most languages support some mechanism of calling a DLL). You can link to class libraries in two ways. The first is to statically bind to the library in such a way as to embed the library within the compiled code. The second method is to bind to the library at runtime, using a call to **LoadLibrary( )**. Both these methods are essentially procedural. The first also suffers from an increased executable size. The second, has little or no versioning capabilities.

While Visual C++ includes built-in support for COM programming, and this support is significantly easier with Visual Studio 7, the bottom line is that programmers are still required to implement **IUnknown**. This also makes creating COM components more complicated.

Memory Management

Little doubt exists that one of the most significant areas of comparison between native C++ and C# is in memory management. More specifically, the fact that *all* heap-allocated memory in C# is managed by the CLR garbage collection algorithm. The result is that each language has various advantages and tradeoffs the developer must consider when selecting which language to code. Because most of this material has already been covered and is discussed further in Chapter 5, we leave this discussion relatively short.

▶ In C++, the developer decides whether structs and class instances are placed on the stack or the heap.

▶ In C++, any heap-allocated data requires an explicit deallocation call. This has been made significantly easier through the use of smart pointers, but it's still one of the leading causes of memory leaks. The responsibility of the C++ programmer to verify that allocation and deallocation calls pair up cannot be understated.

▶ C++ has a high degree of control over when memory is released.

▶ The C# programmer has to abdicate memory deallocation decisions to the garbage collector. In C#, there isn't even a delete keyword to free up memory. (The garbage collector can be manually triggered to run, however.)

▶ C# has no means of supporting automatic finalization when a heap-allocated variable goes out of scope. This inherently results in greater memory usage overall and requires programmers to make a paradigm shift in how they program. (When interfacing with COM+, deterministic finalization can be achieved although restrictions exist.)

▶ C# allocates memory in large chunks. The result is that initialization of data types is extremely fast, as long as the garbage collector doesn't have to run.

▶ Garbage collection freezes execution of all managed threads until it completes.

▶ As previously stated, C# structs are stack allocated and class instances are heap allocated.

▶ C++/COM requires explicit reference counting calls that increase the number of round trips between components.

▶ C++/COM is susceptible to errors by clients outside its control that don't correctly handle reference counting.

▶ To gain direct access to memory in C# requires unsafe and fixed constructs. This is extra programming overhead not required in C++.

Given the length of this list, it should be clear that choosing a language based on memory management alone isn't an easy decision. Software designers need to give careful consideration to their particular application requirements when they select whether or not to write in the managed world.

Performance

Based on the earlier discussion of performance among .NET languages, what we're left with here is a discussion of native C++ applications against .NET applications. You would expect that given the supposed overhead of the .NET runtime, the performance of C++ code to C# code would vary considerably. This doesn't appear to be the case, though. Several performance advantages can be gained in memory management through garbage collection, as discussed in Chapter 3.

There's also the performance of the developer to consider. The programmer is given much less responsibility for things such as memory management, which lets them concentrate on building applications and components, and lets them forget about memory management.

Note, for specific cases where direct memory manipulation is required, native C++ offers an advantage through its built-in support for direct memory manipulation, without requiring unsafe and fixed modifiers. There's no reason to assume at this time that direct memory manipulations will be any faster or slower in either environment. Both will translate the program code into native executable code prior to being compiled.

The one context where native C++ code offers a clear advantage over the managed world is in real-time applications. *Real time* has a broad variety of definitions, so it isn't possible to state unequivocally that C# shouldn't be used to run real-time applications. If program requirements are such that a particular piece of code must execute within a short window of time, however, we recommend avoiding C# and the managed environment. The garbage collector shuts down all managed threads when it runs, and there's no telling when the garbage collector will run, so short execution windows could easily be missed. This problem can be avoided using C++-based unmanaged worker threads.

Comparing C# to Visual Basic.NET

Visual Basic.NET is a completely new version of Visual Basic for the .NET platform. It retains much of the syntax of its predecessor, Visual Basic 6, while introducing significant new functionality, including support for true object-oriented constructs, such as inheritance. For those keeping score at home, what this means is Visual Basic 6 had a major overhaul on its way to becoming Visual Basic.NET or VB.NET. Because VB.NET is Common Language Specification-compliant, it includes support for single object inheritance, structured exception handling (try, catch, and finally), native interface definition, delegates, shared class members, and a set of new operators. With these changes, Visual Basic.NET has gone from being a good "glue" environment for rapid development of Windows GUI applications to a first-class component software development environment. Programmers no longer need to resort to C++-based COM components to write the more challenging portions of their code.

This is a boon to existing Visual Basic programmers who have been requesting these features from Microsoft for years, but it comes at a big price because VB.NET is essentially a new programming language. Microsoft is providing a program that converts existing VB 6 projects to VB.NET but, to truly take advantage of the .NET features and functions such as inheritance, redesigns and rewrites are required.

As is the case with Managed C++ and C#, VB.NET and C# differ primarily in syntax. C# inherits much of its syntax from C and C++, while Visual Basic.NET inherits much of its syntax from Visual Basic 6. Programs of near-equal functionality can be written with either language, but a few significant differences still exist beyond syntax between C# and VB, which are worthy of discussion. That discussion follows.

Built-in Late Binding Support in VB.NET

Visual Basic.NET provides built-in support for late binding to COM objects. For those times when you need it, this can be a significant programmatic savings. To achieve the same result in C# requires manual programming using COM interoperability infrastructure and reflection. This requires significantly more effort than the Visual Basic syntax.

No Support for Operator Overloading

Visual Basic.NET doesn't directly support operator overloading. As such, it cannot officially use or access operators overloaded in languages such as C#. In any event, .NET interoperability guidelines recommend that a type (class or structure) with overloaded operators should also provide companion methods that represent the overloaded operator. For example, if the + operator is overloaded, then an Add( ) method should also be provided. This negates much of the advantages of overloading operators for classes intended to interoperate with other .NET languages like VB.NET.

The following example shows a Visual Basic.NET sample program that uses the Vector struct type from Chapter 2.

```
' Tests the C# vector type
' from Visual Basic.NET
Imports System
Imports CSharpHeadStart

Module EntryPoint
  sub Main()
    Dim v1 as new Vector(1, 1, 1)
    Dim v2 as new Vector(1, 2, 3)

    'no can do
    ' v2 = v1 + v2

    'can do, but officially supported?
    v2 = Vector.op_Addition(v1, v2)

    Console.WriteLine("v1 + v2 = {0}", v2)
  End sub
end module
```

The previous code yields the following results:

```
v1 + v2 = 2,3,4
```

An attempt to execute the commented line of code that adds the vectors together results in a compiler error. The VB compiler doesn't know how to interpret this operator when it's applied to Vectors. The Vector.op_Addition( ) in the next line of code is generated by the C# compiler for the overloaded addition operator. You can see the method names by the C# compiler for overloaded operators by inspecting the program's metadata with ILDASM.EXE.

Using the generated method, instead of a method provided by the type definition, puts your code at the mercy of the C# compiler and any future changes to code generated by the compiler. So, the only question remaining is, if overloaded operators are only supported in a subset of .NET languages and a companion method needs to be provided anyway, what's the real advantage of them?

Safe Mode and Pointers

Visual Basic.NET has no unsafe keyword and no way to define pointers. Any programming requiring direct memory pointers must be done either in unsafe C# or in native C++. Visual Basic does include an **AddressOf** operator, but its use is limited to creating method delegates. Because of .NET's cross-language capability, this isn't that bad because it's easy to define a public class in C# for use in VB.NET.

Arrays

Visual Basic.NET doesn't support the jagged arrays of C#, though it does provide support for dynamically resizing arrays with the **ReDim** statement. A similar result can only be achieved in C# by manually allocating a second array with the new dimensions and copying the contents from the original array to the second. The array class does have copy methods that can be leveraged for this purpose.

This is a good time to point out that the lower bound of all arrays in Visual Basic.NET is 0. An experienced Visual Basic programmer might have assumed that flexible bounding of arrays in Visual Basic was an advantage but, alas, it isn't. This allows public VB arrays to easily interoperate with other languages, but this is also a good example of "least common denominator" design.

switch vs. Select Case

VB.NET's **Select Case** evaluates a select expression against a series of case statement expressions while C#'s **switch** matches an integral or string expression to a list of constant expressions. VB.NET's support of case statement expressions, as opposed to constants, yields the possibility for much richer select statements than is achievable in C#. Similar to C#, VB.NET also supports transfer of control within a statement block using **goto**, but a label is required. Both languages prevent case fall through, however. In the case of C#, an explicit flow control statement, such as a break, is required, while in VB, the statement block simply stops executing.

Consider the following VB.NET sample:

```
Imports System

Module Module1
  Sub Main()
    Dim favoriteLanguage As String

    Do While True

      Console.Write("> ")
      favoriteLanguage = Console.ReadLine()
      If favoriteLanguage = "" Then
        Exit Do
      End If

      Select Case favoriteLanguage
        Case "C#", "CSharp"
          Console.WriteLine("C# is music to my ears")
        Case "C"
          Console.WriteLine("I ain't got no stinkin class")
          Goto here
        Case "C++"
here:
          Console.WriteLine("-> shows the way to go")
        Case "VB", "Visual Basic"
        Case "A" To "z"
          Console.WriteLine("Dim is not so dull")
        Case Else
          Console.WriteLine(_
            "We are not talking French and German here")
      End Select
    Loop
  End Sub
End Module
```

In the previous sample, we can express a range of matches using the To statement. The amount of code required to do this with C#'s switch statement would make using it alone impractical. An if( ) inside the default case is required to handle the range checking. The C# if( ) version included in the following helps to illustrate what's happening in the VB To.

```
default:
  if ((String.Compare("A", inputString) <= 0)
    && (String.Compare("z", inputString) >= 0))
    Console.WriteLine("Dim is not so dull");
  else
    Console.WriteLine(
      "We are not talking French and German here");
  break;
}
```

With Blocks in VB.NET

We end our VB comparison with a minor syntax convenience. VB.NET supports namespaces just like C# but, over and above namespaces, **With** and **End With** can be used in Visual Basic to support inline short cuts to objects references. No construct is comparable to **With** in C#. The following lists a brief example:

```
Imports System

Class SimpleClass
  Sub SimpleSub()
    Console.WriteLine("simple sub")
  End Sub
End Class

Module EntryPoint
  Sub Main()
    Dim mySimpleClass as New SimpleClass

    With mySimpleClass
      .SimpleSub
    End With

  End Sub
End Module
```

This statement comes in especially handy when doing a large number of interactions with the same class, for example, when loading or retrieving data from a record set.

Comparing C# to Java

Now that we've compared C# to C++ and Visual Basic, we'll turn our attention to Java. This section concentrates on a comparison of the languages, but it wouldn't be complete without some discussion of the Java platform as well. Like C#, much of what Java is about is derived from the software platform it runs on, the Java Virtual Machine (JVM) and the Java Foundation Class library.

Java's goals are to provide a simple, robust, object-oriented, secure, easy to deploy, cross-platform environment for users building component-based software. These goals are consistent with the goals of C# and the .NET Framework.

Both C# and Java are language descendants of C++. At the same time, both C# and Java make significant changes to C++ in order to simplify programming. This simplification is achieved through features such as garbage-collected runtimes, single-file construction semantics, tight type checking, lack of header files, and the lack of requiring forward declarations of classes. The bottom line is less Java or C# code class is required to perform similar functions than C++, and less code to perform the same function is a good thing no matter how you look at it.

Both languages support single inheritance with "object" at the root of their object hierarchies, providing rich built-in string types as well. Objects (nonprimitive types) are allocated on the heap using the new operator and are garbage collected by their respective runtimes. Both have extensive class libraries to support the language.

All code is written in classes and neither global variables nor global functions are supported. Static class data and methods are provided, however, which allows what would otherwise be disconnected sets of methods and data to be defined in classes.

Java compiles to intermediate byte codes that are loaded and executed by the JVM. While the initial design for Java was as an interpreted language, Just-In-Time (JIT) compilers have been an option for quite some time. As we've discussed already, C# compiles to Intermediate Language (IL) which is loaded, Just In Time compiled and executed by the .NET Common Language Runtime. No interpreted mode exists for IL at the current time.

With the help of intermediate language, which is platform-independent, programs can be automatically deployed to clients simply by copying the programs to the client. This assumes, of course, that the required runtime is already loaded and the program requires no special services.

Because the runtime environment executes all code, it also provides access to system resources and can, therefore, tightly control access to those resources. In fact, one of the strongest initial selling points of Java was it didn't allow direct access to local resources and, therefore, was far more secure than ActiveX technologies for doing Web deployment. The bottom-line requirement of the runtime is that applications must be granted access to system resources. In addition to this, assuming a solid runtime environment, there should be no way for a program to crash the system. It may well fail for a variety of reasons, but a hard crash should never happen.

Metadata is accessible via reflection interfaces in both C# and Java. Code can be loaded and executed using reflection interfaces in both environments. Chapter 3 has a detailed discussion of .NET reflection. Java's reflection APIs support similar capabilities for navigating the classes, and their fields and methods, as well as providing a mechanism to invoke methods via **java.lang.reflect.Method.invoke( )**. Java doesn't include the capability to define custom attributes.

C# and Java both support automatic generation of documentation from source code, though they achieve this using slightly different methods. C# uses comments with XML-based tags and Java uses comments with special attributes. In C#, the compiler generates the output XML file via the **/out** command, while Java uses a separate Javadoc utility that invokes the Java compiler. The **Javadoc** tool produces HTML output, whereas the C# tool produces XML. The base requirement for class documentation is nicely satisfied with the ready-made HTML output produced by **Javadoc**.

One of Java's stated goals is to be cross-platform. Java has already largely met this goal in that the Java runtime is available for a large number of platforms above and beyond Windows, including Unix, Macintosh, and Linux, as well as mobile and network computing platforms. Before jumping to the conclusion that Microsoft's goals are not cross-platform or that their only desire is to run .NET on Windows platforms, consider that .NET does provide open platform services that target both multiple clients and language neutrality. At least part of the reason for submitting C# and the Common Language Runtime to ECMA for standardization is to facilitate the development of these technologies on other platforms. At a minimum, both Microsoft and Sun have serious intentions on gaining market share in mobile and embedded platforms, including portable phones, PDAs, set top boxes, and the obligatory toasters with their respective platforms.

With all the good intentions of cross-platform compatibility or the "Write Once and Run Anywhere" ideal of Java, Java is not a completely open platform. Essentially all code that runs on a virtual machine must be written in Java, and, gaining access to services not provided by the Java runtime requires significant programming effort.

Packages, Namespaces, Assemblies, Source Files, and Versioning

Java packages have attributes of both .NET assemblies and C# namespaces. Packages contain all the distribution code and configuration required for an application or library. The import directive in a Java program dictates the location of a package, while in C#, the using directive only provides a hint as to the actual structure or location of the assemblies. The separation of the logical namespace from the physical layout in C# keeps all packaging and directory location issues out of the source code.

An advantage the C# and .NET assembly concept have over packages is that multiple versions of the same assembly can be installed and running at the same time on the same machine. Java packages essentially require that classes be placed into a directory specific to the package and the source code dictates which package gets loaded. The same effect as .NET assemblies could be achieved by changing source code, but that isn't an attractive alternative.

At the source level, the convention for Java is to put one public class in each file and, in fact, some compilers require this. C# allows any source file arrangement the developer might find desirable or convenient.

Primitive Types

The base primitive types supplied by Java are effectively the same as value types in C#, however, they're implemented a bit differently. In C#, all value types are derived from objects, whereas, in Java, the primitive types are special. Wrapper classes are provided for each primitive type, so they can be treated like objects; however, as objects, they can no longer be treated like primitive types. C# provides the automatic boxing and unboxing technique to move the value types between value and reference as needed and, therefore, allows the value type operator semantics to be maintained with little or no effort. In Java, this transformation must be performed manually using the appropriate wrapper class.

Java doesn't provide for operator overloading, so a type (class) you define in Java cannot look or act much like a primitive type. Finally, C# supports a struct type and Java doesn't.

The Java Integer object (as opposed to the int type), for example, cannot be used to do arithmetic, which would be possible if Java supported operator overloading. C#'s "everything is an object" approach provides great convenience. The same boxing and unboxing approach could be taken in Java, but it must be built by hand by the developer and will have a less functional result.

Class Definition and Usage

Although classes are defined and used in essentially the same way in C# and Java, a few noteworthy differences exist. In Java, class members are virtual by default and a method having the same name in a derived class overrides the base member. In C#, the base member is required to have the virtual keyword and the derived member is required to use the override keyword. An attempt to hide a base member without specifying override results in a warning and an attempt to hide a base nonvirtual base member result in a compiler error unless the **new** modifier is used. **New** has no complement in Java. The other issue with the Java approach is that calling a virtual function is a bit slower than calling a nonvirtual function because a virtual call cannot be resolved until runtime, while a nonvirtual function can be resolved at compile time.

Some differences also occur when declaring member access. Reviewing the C# access rules provided in Chapter 2 might help before proceeding here because the same keywords have different meaning, even though the end result is similar. Java supports public, protected, private, and package access for class members, and the access modifiers apply to the classes, not to the instances themselves. This makes a difference with private access, which is virtually identical to private access in C#, except a class instance can access private members of other instances of the same class. An example is included in the following. Public access is identical to C#. Protected access in Java is effectively the same as C#'s **internal protected**, except a Java derived class outside the assembly cannot directly access the protected class members inside the assembly. Lastly, package access, which you get in Java by not specifying an access modifier, is the same as **internal** in C#. The only difference here is C# enables you to specify internal access explicitly, while Java leaves it as the default when no other access modifier is provided.

In Java, access in subclasses can be expanded, but not reduced. In other words, protected access can be turned into public, but not into private. C# doesn't allow this. An attempt to expand an access modifier in a derived class results in a compile error.

As mentioned previously, Java access levels apply to the class and not to the instances, which means private properties are accessible from within other objects of the same type. In C#, no access to private variables is allowed outside the class definition and its current instance. This is illustrated in the following Java class definition:

```
class MyPrivate
{
  private int privateVar = 5;
  public void ToString() {
    System.out.println(privateVar);
  }
  public MyPrivate(int InitialVar){
    privateVar = InitialVar;
  }
  public int getVar() {
    return privateVar;
  }
  public boolean CompareVar(MyPrivate mp){
    return this.privateVar == mp.privateVar;
  }
}
```

The **CompareVar( )** method of the **MyPrivate** class uses another instance of
MyPrivate to verify if the objects' private variables are the same. An attempt to do
this same operation in C# will be rejected by the compiler.

Delegates and Events

C# provides built-in delegates and events. Java uses interfaces and inner class
definitions to achieve a similar result. C# delegates, by their nature, support a
single-method call, while interfaces require an all or nothing approach. All methods
of an interface must be implemented. For example, in the Java AWT, a class can
implement the **MouseListener** interface to handle mouse events. Even if you only
care about one of the events, however, you're obligated by the interface contract to
implement all five of the methods declared by the **MouseListener** interface, even if
they do nothing. This is demonstrated in the following code sample that implements
a simple Java applet, which responds to mouse events by displaying a message
wherever the mouse button was clicked.

```java
import java.applet.*;
import java.awt.*;
import java.awt.event.*;

public class MouseTest extends Applet implements MouseListener {
  private int mouseX;
  private int mouseY;

  public void init() {
    addMouseListener(this);
  }

  public void paint(Graphics g) {
      g.drawString("moused!", mouseX, mouseY);
  }

  public void mousePressed(MouseEvent event) {
      mouseX = event.getX();
      mouseY = event.getY();
      repaint();
  }
  public void mouseClicked(MouseEvent event) {}
  public void mouseReleased(MouseEvent event) {}
  public void mouseEntered(MouseEvent event) {}
  public void mouseExited(MouseEvent event) {}
}
```

The **init( )** event, which is the first one called by the Java runtime, adds the current listener, while the **mousePressed( )** method implements the handler for that event. Notice the other four mouse-handler routines that must be declared to satisfy the interface contract.

A better approach than directly implementing interfaces for this would be to use adapter classes. *Adapter classes* are base classes that implement the defined interface and are generally provided by the server. The client derives a new inner class from the adapter class to avoid having to explicitly implement all the events' interfaces. In the case of **MouseEvents**, the adapter class is **MouseAdapter** and it includes virtual methods for each of the mouse events. You then override only the methods you're interested in. This is a much cleaner approach, but whether it's as clean as the C# delegates is debatable. At a minimum, this approach requires the server class to provide the adaptors, as well as the interface. The following shows the adapter-based implementation:

```java
import java.applet.*;
import java.awt.*;
import java.awt.event.*;

public class MouseTestA extends Applet {
  private int mouseX;
  private int mouseY;

  public void init() {
    addMouseListener(new MyMouseAdapter());
  }

  public void paint(Graphics g) {
     g.drawString("moused!", mouseX, mouseY);
  }

  class MyMouseAdapter extends MouseAdapter {
    public void mousePressed(MouseEvent event) {
       mouseX = event.getX();
       mouseY = event.getY();
       repaint();
    }
  }
}
```

Generally speaking, if the server requires multiple methods—something beyond a simple method call—or if the server expects or requires multiple methods, then an interface should be used, even in C#. In the case of the **MouseListener**, you become registered for five different events by adding one listener. If the server only needs one method call and expects many clients, however, then interfaces can add needless overhead.

Another point worthy of noting is that the C# delegate and C# (.NET) multicast delegate are already built to handle invoking the delegates. Using interfaces, a server needs to provide its own invocation code, though implementing a collection of connected objects supporting the interface, and calling the connected objects at the appropriate time isn't that big a deal.

Passing Parameters by Reference

Java method parameters can only be passed by value. Because all Java types, except its primitive types, are derived from the base object type, this is a non-issue, except for when a method would like to change the value of a primitive type or it would like to change an object reference (point an object reference variable at a different object). When that situation occurs, the client must manually "box" the value in an object. One easy way to do this is by using an array. The downside is, for certain applications, this can cause a significant performance hit. As already discussed, in C#, an integer can be passed by reference directly with no boxing required.

Properties

C# includes native support for properties, Java doesn't. In Java, a consumer of the class has additional get/set pairs of methods to call, while the consumer of the C# class simply uses the property as if it were a field. So, if you have a boolean property, **getBooleanProperty( )** and **setBooleanProperty( )** methods are needed. (Because this is boolean, the get access methods might be written as is **BooleanProperty( )** instead.)

On the surface, you might wonder what the big deal is. While properties in C# aren't world-changing, they are another example of where things are made explicit in C#. The metadata for the class clearly spells out what the purpose is of a given field, making it easier to consume. Imagine a class with ten properties. In C#, the documentation for the class definition lists the ten properties. In Java, the class definition lists 20 methods, one for each get and set method on the class. What's left to naming convention and style in Java is enforced by the compiler in C#.

Enumerations

Java doesn't directly support enumerations, though enumerations can be simulated using constant fields defined in a class definition or on an interface. In contrast, the C# enumerated type allows for tighter type checking, type consumption by editors (intelli-sense), and better readability. Any good class definition includes appropriate enumerations for method parameters because this aids the productivity of users of the class. The enumerations in C# are easier to document and the intention is clear. With Java, you need at least to pause for a second and consider the intention of the class. To be fair, this last point could be overcome within a project by following a decent naming convention, but there's no guarantee other third parties won't come up with their own convention, reducing the usefulness of the nameing convention in the first place.

If you rewrite your simple enumeration from the Language Overview section in Java, you need to define a class (or an interface) and declare constants using the **final** keyword. The code would look like this:

```
class TheWays {
  public final static int North = 1;
  public final static int South = 2;
  public final static int East = 3;
  public final static int West = 4;
  public final static int ToSanJose = West;
}

class enums {
  public static void main (String args[]) {
    System.out.println(
      "The way to san jose is " + TheWays.ToSanJose);
  }
}
```

This program yields the output as follows:

```
The way to san jose is 4
```

So, the code isn't as straightforward, is less descriptive in terms of the metadata, and yields an integer result, instead of a string result when using default output. As was shown in the C# enumeration sample in the Language Overview section, the metadata carries the enumeration text, so when you execute the corresponding C# code, you get a string result.

```
Console.WriteLine("The way is {0}", way);
```

This sample produces the following results:

```
The way is West.
```

C# Unsafe Mode

Java has no such thing as "unsafe mode" or an "address of" operator. So, such things as direct memory manipulations aren't possible in native Java. To achieve the same functionality requires you go outside the environment with Java Native Interfaces (JNI). Unsafe mode defeats some of the purpose of what Java is about, so it's not surprising it isn't supported. However, lack of an unsafe mode also rules out Java as a development platform for when it is required.

Indexers

Java doesn't have any complement to C# indexers. As described in the Language Overview, indexers provide array-like access to a class. This could be considered a relatively minor inconvenience because the Java code to replace indexers would simply be to add explicit indexing methods.

Specifying Thrown Exceptions

Both C# and Java support the **try**, **catch**, and **finally** approach for handling errors and both support user-defined exceptions and throwing exceptions. The difference comes into play where C# enables you to throw an exception from anywhere without specifying it ahead of time. Java requires any non-runtime exceptions to be thrown by a method, or any method called by the method, to be declared in the method header.

```
class MyErrorProneClass throws ThisException, ThatException {
  try {

  }

  catch {

  }
  finally {

  }
}
```

At first, this may seem unnecessarily harsh on the programmer because it seems to require the help of a fortune-teller for many cases. Remember, the methods called in the **try** block also have to publish which errors they will be throwing. If the method implementation doesn't catch them, it will be throwing them even if it doesn't do so explicitly. Having this extra information in the metadata of the class is helpful, but it's debatable if this is worth the extra effort. This doesn't make handling exceptions easier and, in some cases, it may lead programmers away from implementing them.

Arrays

In C#, arrays may be rectangular or jagged, while in Java, all multidimensioned arrays are jagged. Rectangular arrays can be more efficiently accessed because a member can be looked up directly using a simple calculation. With a jagged array, a separate lookup is required for each dimension of the array.

Interfaces

Both Java and C# support the concept of an interface. A few differences worth noting are in their definition and use, however. C# doesn't allow type definitions in interfaces, while a Java interface definition can include constant type data. In C#, you can implement explicit (fully qualified) interface methods. This technique can be used if duplicate methods are found on multiple interfaces or if one wishes to hide the implementation of an interface from public use.

The switch Statement

In Java, the **switch** statement can only be controlled by an integer, while C# supports an integral or string expression. In addition, the C# **switch** statement prevents fall through from case to case. If more than one case is appropriate, a goto is required.

The foreach Statement

C# includes the **foreach** statement for quick and easy iterating over collections or, said another way, any object that supports the **IEnumerable** interface. In Java, collection iteration must be done either with a **for** loop or a **while** construct.

CHAPTER 5

Working Within the Bounds of C#

IN THIS CHAPTER:

Deterministic Finalization

Multiple Inheritance

Macros

Templates

Source Code Security

Despite the power of C# and the careful attention its engineers paid in designing a language with a robust set of features, alert readers will have noticed it isn't perfect, and C# has some language features missing. In this chapter, we discuss several items that aren't part of the language and yet are considered "features" in other languages.

In reading the following discussions, readers shouldn't expect to find any silver-bullet solutions that have absolutely no cost or drawback. This chapter discusses the shortcomings and proposes possible workarounds, when available. None of the solutions are perfect, however. Perhaps knowing the C# engineers neglected to include the features directly indicates significant caveats existed. That said, hopefully, a greater understanding of the issues will enable you to better leverage the language to your advantage, even in those areas where it falls short of meeting your expectations.

Before we begin examining each item, let's consider briefly that, for some, a so-called shortcoming is actually a feature. For example, some developers believe multiple-inheritance is actually a bad characteristic to support in a language because of the potential that it could be abused. For these readers, there's little point in discussing workarounds for features they believe shouldn't be there in the first place. For the most part, however, the features missing from C# are found in C++. And, because C# is designed as the language of choice for C++ programmers who want to write managed code, at least discussing possible solutions that can be used in addressing the C# shortcomings seems important.

Deterministic Finalization

The first feature lacking from C# to consider is deterministic finalization. As covered in Chapter 4, deterministic finalization is generally understood as the calling of any finalization code immediately before all references to it have been removed. In the context of our discussion here, *deterministic finalization* is the action of calling a class's "clean-up" code automatically, deterministically, and reliably.

► Automatically: For finalization to be automatic, programmers shouldn't have to make calls explicitly to execute finalization code. For example, programmers shouldn't have to call the destructor method explicitly on a class. With .NET, the garbage collector automatically calls destructor, so "automatically" is supported in .NET.

▶ Deterministically: For finalization to occur deterministically, it needs to occur at a specific time in the code execution sequence. Looking at a block of code and knowing specifically between what two portions of code finalization will occur should be possible. In the managed environment, this isn't the case, however. All that's known is finalization code will run sometime after the class is no longer referenced. Furthermore, the order in which the finalization code will be called isn't known. Given class A contains class B, no guarantee exists that finalization code in class B will be called before finalization code in class A (or vice versa). To achieve deterministic finalization in .NET, a programmer needs to make a call explicitly to the finalization code.

NOTE

Deterministic finalization means determining at compile time the specific location in the code at which finalization will occur.

▶ Reliably: For finalization to be reliable, it should "always" be called. Given the algorithm of the garbage collector, as described in Chapter 3, we can assume the CLR will call all objects that have **Finalize( )** methods because they'll be added to the freachable queue before the garbage collector cleans them up. This makes the finalization reasonably reliable, (only "reasonably" reliable because it isn't called in the event of unhandled exceptions, computer crashes, significant natural disasters, and that sort of thing).

The .NET environment essentially supports two of the three criteria for deterministic finalization: Automatically and Reliably.

To understand this a little more fully, consider deterministic finalization in C++ or Visual Basic 6.0 (VB 6.0). Of these two, Visual Basic is the one that fully supports automatic finalization. C++ only natively supports automatic finalization on classes that are allocated on the stack. Heap allocated classes require a specific call to **delete**. Fortunately, in the C++ case, wrappers can be written (usually using templates) that automatically invoke the calls to **delete**. In both languages, the finalization is deterministic. Finalization occurs at the instance a stack-allocated variable goes out of scope. Last, in both languages, finalization is reasonably reliable. Tearing out the processor or not handling an exception skirts the calling of finalization but, presumably, these are rare occasions.

Note, in our discussions of deterministic finalization, we are discussing *resource* cleanup, rather than *memory* cleanup. Given the mechanics of the .NET garbage collection algorithm, we generally do not need to worry about the specifics of memory management. The garbage collector uses whatever memory is available on the system and appropriately reduces its use as other applications start and take up memory resources. In other words, the garbage collector uses a system's memory to its full capacity and automatically adjusts as memory capacity changes.

Rather than memory per se, what deterministic finalization is concerned with (at least in the context of this discussion) are the expensive resources a class may have accumulated during its lifetime. Resource cleanup is generally more time-sensitive than memory cleanup, hence, the emphasis on *deterministic* finalization. One example of an expensive resource that requires cleanup could be a shared log file. If the file was opened for exclusive access, then no other applications could access the file until the resource was released. A second example could be a mutex or semaphore that prevents concurrent access to a section of code. It's critical that the semaphore be released immediately following the section of code on which synchronization is required. If not, the application runs less efficiently. This is especially important for locks on database resources, such as tables and records. In general, finalization code is concerned with cleaning up expensive resources or resources that become expensive if held beyond the time required.

Releasing Resources Explicitly

The simplest method for implementing deterministic finalization in the .NET framework is simply to clean up resources manually. This method makes the most sense when the allocation of resources can occur within the same function as the deallocation of those resources. For example, consider the **Monitor** class, which is the .NET version of a semaphore. It's important for every call to **Monitor.Enter( )** to be balanced with a call to **Monitor.Exit( )**. Because **Monitor** is generally used to provide synchronization to a section of code within one function, it's relatively easy to maintain the balance between **Enter( )** and **Exit( )** calls. Programmers simply form a habit of always coding the **Exit( )** call at the same time the **Enter( )** call is coded in the same manner that they tend to pair up curly braces. By explicitly calling **Exit( )**, a programmer is adding *deterministic* finalization.

Although the explicit release of resources by calling **Exit( )** is deterministic, unfortunately, manually making the call (by definition) isn't automatic. Furthermore, to make the call reliable, a **try-catch-finally** block should surround the entire section of code from the **Enter( )** to the **Exit( )** so, even if an exception occurs, the **Exit( )** is still called. To help out in writing the **try-catch-finally** block, C# provides the special **lock** syntax.

Variable Declaration with the using Keyword

To deterministically, reliably, and "pseudoautomatically" free up local function variables, C# provides a special syntax as the following shows.

```
using (TempFile tempFile = new tempFile ())
{
  // Do something
  . . .
}
```

C# takes the **using** keyword and automatically generates equivalent IL code that essentially mimics the following C# code:

```
TempFile tempFile = new TempFile();
try {
  // Do something
  . . .
}
finally {
    if (tempFile != null) ((IDisposable)tempFile).Dispose();
}
```

What does the **using** statement really offer? At its core, the **using** statement simply reduces the amount of typing you have to do. Essentially, it serves as a glorified macro, converting your code so it's deterministically and reliably finalized: deterministically because finalization code (**Dispose( )**) is called at a known time, and reliably because it's called from inside a **finally** block.

A few caveats do exist, though. First, nothing prevents you from passing a reference to the class outside the scope of the function, thereby essentially setting up a situation in which **Dispose( )** is called before all references to the variable are removed. Second, because nothing is enforcing the use of the **using** keyword when declaring your class, developers could easily neglect to call **Dispose( )**. This is why the term "pseudoautomatically" was previously used. If a programmer reads the documentation and remembers to declare a class variable with the **using** keyword (or writes the **try-catch** block manually), then deterministic finalization is automatic. Neglecting the keyword, however, results in a nondeterministic call to any finalization code (assuming the destructor method was, indeed, implemented in the class). One last thing to note about the **using** keyword is this: variables declared within the resource acquisition section of the **using** statement (the section inside the **using** parentheses) are read only.

NOTE

*To summarize, the **using** keyword provides a means of automatically generating a call to a **Dispose( )** method before a local function variable goes out of scope.*

Notice that for the **using** syntax to compile, your class (**TempFile( )** in the following example) must implement the **System.IDisposable** interface. This interface has only one method, **Dispose( )**, which takes no parameters and returns a **void**. (**System.IDisposable** wasn't defined until Beta 2.) In general, always implementing the **System.IDisposable** interface on any classes that require resource cleanup is considered good practice. This provides a standard means for recognizing when resource management is required. The obvious implication is if you use a class that supports the **System.IDisposable** interface, you must be sure to call its **Dispose( )** method (or use the **using** keyword) as soon as the class is no longer needed. Another good practice is to stop the garbage collector from calling the destructor method because it's assumed any code the finalize method would execute has already been run by the **Dispose( )** method. To prevent the destructor from being called again, use the **System.GC.SuppressFinalize( )** method. By removing the call to the destructor method, you reduce the overhead involved with adding another class to the freachable queue.

NOTE

*Developers should implement the **System.IDisposable** interface on all classes where they want deterministic resource cleanup to be performed. Programmers who use a class that implements the **System.IDisposable** interface should call its **Dispose( )** method as soon as the classes' resources are no longer needed. Or, the class should be declared with the **using** keyword, assuming no additional references are being created outside the scope of the **using** keyword.*

The following code shows a sample class that implements the **System.IDisposable** interface.

```
namespace CSharpHeadStart
{
  using System;
  using System.IO;

  public class FileStreamResource : FileStream, IDisposable
  {

    ...

    // Just in case Dispose is not called explicitly
    // by the client.
    ~ FileStreamResource()
    {
      Dispose();
    }

    // **********
    // IDisposable
    public void Dispose()
    {
      this.Close();
      // Turn off the call to Finalize() by the GC.
      GC.SuppressFinalize(this);
      // Call base.Dispose() if implemented.
    }
    ...
  }
  ...
}
```

Notice, despite the fact that the **IDisposable** interface has been implemented, a destructor declaration still exists (which is compiled to a **Finalize( )** method in IL). This provides a backup for calling **Dispose( )** if a client neglects to do so explicitly.

Reference Counting

If the **using** keyword provides a method for generating code to call the **Dispose( )** method on a local function variable, what can programmers do for the case in which variables are passed beyond the scope of a function call and end up having multiple references? If multiple references are created, how can it be determined when to release any expensive resources held by the referenced object?

In these cases, you're required to fall back on the same techniques that were such an integral part of COM. Essentially, you need to add some type of reference counting. The code follows:

```
namespace CSharpHeadStart.ReferenceCounting
{
  public interface IRefCounted
  {
    void AddRef();
    void Release();
  }

  // More stuff to be defined here later
  ...
}

namespace CSharpHeadStart
{
  using System;
  using System.IO;
  using ReferenceCounting;
  using System.Diagnostics;

  public class FileStreamRefCounted :
    FileStream, IDisposable, IRefCounted
  {

    ...

    // Just in case Dispose is not called explicitly
    // by the client.
    ~FileStreamRefCounted()
```

```
  {
    Dispose();
  }

  // ***********
  // IDisposable
  public void Dispose()
  {
    this.Close();
    CheckReferenceCount();
    // Turn off the call to Finalize() by the GC.
    GC.SuppressFinalize(this);
    // Call base.Dispose() if implemented.
  }

  // ***********
  // IRefCounted
  // Initialize to one so AddRef() call not required
  // upon instantiation of class.
  protected int referenceCount = 1;
  public void AddRef()
  {
    referenceCount++;
  }
  public void Release()
  {
    referenceCount--;
    if(referenceCount == 0)
    {
      Dispose();
    }
    return;
  }

  [Conditional("DEBUG")]
  protected virtual void CheckReferenceCount()
  {
    System.Diagnostics.Debug.Assert((referenceCount == 0),
      "Reference handling was not performed correctly for "
      + ToString(),
      "Reference count is " + referenceCount.ToString());
  }
}
}
```

The first thing to note in the previous code listing is **FileStreamRefCounted** now implements one more interface, **IRefCounted**. **IRefCounted** declares the reference counting methods to be placed on classes that require resource cleanup via reference counting. (At press time, there was no standard **IRefCounted** interface.) Let's look at **IRefCounted**'s implementation.

The first thing to note is the reference counting variable, **referenceCount**, is initialized to one. When instantiated, it's assumed the class will have one reference, so this is set automatically. Although calling **AddRef( )** from inside the **FileStreamRefCounted** constructors is possible, so many constructors must be overridden, this is impractical. Instead, the reference-counting field is initialized automatically. Setting the reference count to one at instantiation follows the model established by COM; in other words, COM's **CoCreateInstance( )** or **CoCreateInstanceEx( )** returns an object whose reference count is one. This also forces programmers into an awareness of reference counting in debug builds because if **Release( )** isn't called at least once, an assert occurs.

Next, comes the implementation for **AddRef( )** and **Release( )**. **AddRef( )** bumps the reference count, while **Release( )** decrements it. In the **Release( )** function, **Dispose( )** is called when the reference count reaches 0. Neither **AddRef( )** nor **Release( )** use synchronization. The general philosophy in .NET classes is only to include synchronization code when required and, instead, to rely on instance variables that aren't shared among multiple requests. This is because synchronization reduces performance, which is needless when only a single thread accesses the class. To convert the code to being thread safe, use the **Interlocked** class as shown in the following:

```
public void AddRef()
{
  Interlocked.Increment(ref referenceCount);
}
public void Release()
{
  if(Interlocked.Decrement(ref referenceCount) == 0)
  {
    Dispose();
  }
}
```

The last significant aspect of the reference count implementation is that **CheckReferenceCount( )** is called if **DEBUG** is defined to help insure reference counting is used correctly and the object always ends with a reference count of zero.

What are the advantages and disadvantages of reference counting? First, the disadvantages: for reference counting to work, all clients are required to make and balance calls to **AddRef( )** and **Release( )** each time new references are created or destroyed. Unfortunately, nothing is enforcing that these calls are made, and the only indication they should be called (aside from any documentation that may accompany the class) is the implementation of the **IRefCounted** (or equivalent) interface and the existence of the two reference-counting methods on the class. Reference counting requires careful attention to make sure every call to **AddRef( )** has a corresponding **Release( )** call. Inevitably, at times, one or the other of these calls will be missing and resources will be released prematurely or not until the garbage collector runs.

NOTE

*Reference counting requires careful attention to make sure every call to **AddRef( )** has a corresponding **Release( )** call.*

Although this is probably negligible for in-process calls, another issue with reference counting is it could significantly decrease performance when calls are required to cross process or network boundaries. The same issue existed in COM, however, and the abundance of COM applications both distributed and local, indicate performance is reasonable.

.NET Finalization

Before we leave the topic of deterministic finalization, it's worth pointing out that even though methods exist to introduce deterministic finalization into your classes, the best method is to avoid requiring it in the first place. In other words, before you begin trying all types of antics to force deterministic finalization into .NET (as I, Mark, did) the first solution is to accept the fact that garbage collection, even garbage collection without deterministic finalization, is good and preferable in the vast majority of cases. This is sometimes more difficult for C++ programmers to accept because of the extensive use of destructors within their C++ classes. However, you must realize that much of the code within C++ destructors was required to deallocate resources (balancing **new** with **delete**) and, without destructors, allocated memory would inevitably result in memory leaks. In contrast, .NET automatically deallocates the memory resources for you. You may not know exactly when this will occur, but you do know it will occur. Furthermore, given a destructor function, .NET automatically cleans up any resources you identify in the destructor function.

NOTE

Garbage collection, even garbage collection without deterministic finalization, is good and preferable to manual memory management in the vast majority of cases.

In some sense, it could be argued that deterministic destruction is, in fact, too restrictive because it forces cleanup at a particular time, even if at that time memory is abundant and processing time is scarce. In other words, .NET memory management can be more efficient than its C++ counterpart in some circumstances. The bottom line is programmers switching to .NET are well advised to accept the fact that deterministic finalization isn't natively present in the managed world and not to worry about the theoretical cases where it could possibly be required until they encounter a real situation where they need it. Although some tradeoffs exist in having automatic memory management, the benefits outweigh the costs in the majority of applications. This isn't a declaration that the .NET garbage collection will solve all the problems in the world (including world hunger), however. It's fully recognized that, at times, you require some type of deterministic finalization; otherwise, what would have been the point of this entire section?

NOTE

The bottom line is programmers switching to .NET are well advised to accept the fact that deterministic finalization isn't natively present in the managed world and not to worry about the cases where it could possibly be required until they encounter a real situation where they need it.

NOTE

Although some tradeoffs exist to having automatic memory management, the benefits outweigh the costs in the majority of applications.

Multiple Inheritance

C# doesn't support multiple inheritance because the feature doesn't exist in the CLR. This becomes obvious when you realize Managed C++ doesn't include the feature either. Before we delve into the details of how to overcome the fact that there's no multiple inheritance, let's consider the seriousness of the problem.

ATL was essentially developed for COM programmers, so they didn't have to hand code implementation of all the interfaces required by a basic component. Toward this end, multiple inheritance was key because each interface a component was required to support was added to the list of classes from which a component was derived. More specifically, an *implementation* class for each of the required interfaces was added to the list of classes the component inherited. Hence, multiple inheritance was integral to the success of ATL.

In C#, the situation has changed significantly because much of the support for standard interfaces in COM has been built into a class's most basic functionality. For example, error handling, class info, and events don't require any special interfaces at all. Even such features as persistence become trivial in .NET because of attributes (see **SerializableAttribute** in the documentation). The result is this: for many of the situations in ATL where multiple inheritance was crucial, it's no longer required in C# and, in fact, no inheritance is required. This doesn't eliminate all scenarios, but it certainly reduces them significantly.

ATLs Multiple Inheritance In-depth

To emphasize the need for multiple inheritance in ATL, lets consider some of the ATL details when multiple inheritance is used. For example, a COM component must support the **IUnknown** interface (by definition) and to do this requires adding **CComObjectRootEx<>** as a parent class to the component class definition. This provided the component with the capability to handle **QueryInterface( )** and support reference counting. Next, if the component is to handle calls from scripting languages, support for the **IDispatch** interface is added by deriving from **IDispatchImpl**. As if this isn't enough, most components need to support **IErrorInfo, IProvideClassInfo, IPersist,** and/or **IConnectionPointContainer** at some point, and each of these has its own implementation classes to be derived from. The fact is, much of the power of ATL is because of multiple inheritance. To support a new interface requires simply adding the implementation class as a parent to the component. This works, not only for standard interfaces for which Microsoft provides implementation classes, but also for any custom interfaces developers want to include in multiple components. In other words, if you need to support some custom interface on multiple components, you can write your own class that implements the interface.

Containment

The first solution to implementing multiple inheritance is to use containment. Let's consider an example. In the previous section, you learned that to implement some type of deterministic destruction when multiple references are created, you need to include two reference-counting methods. However, if you had to rewrite the same method over and over again every time you encounter a scenario where reference counting was required, this would be ridiculous. Therefore, in our example, we'll create an **RefCountedImpl** class designed to implement reference counting. Because we're deriving our class from **System.FileStream**, however, we cannot also inherit **RefCountedImpl**. Instead, we use containment as the following shows. To begin, let's write the **RefCountedImpl** class, so it can generically handle reference counting. A listing of the code follows:

```
namespace CSharpHeadStart.ReferenceCounting
{
  using System.Threading;
  using System;
  using System.Diagnostics;

  public interface IRefCounted
  {
    void AddRef();
    void Release();
  }

  public sealed class RefCountedImpl : IRefCounted
  {
    private long referenceCount = 1;
    private IDisposable refCountObject;

#if DEBUG
    ~RefCountedImpl()
    {
      CheckReferenceCount();
    }

    private void CheckReferenceCount()
    {
      System.Diagnostics.Debug.Assert((referenceCount == 0),
```

```
                "Reference handling was not performed correctly for "
                + refCountObject.ToString(),
                "Reference count is " + referenceCount.ToString());
    }
#endif //DEBUG

    public RefCountedImpl(IDisposable ReferenceCountedObject)
    {
      refCountObject = ReferenceCountedObject;
    }

    public void AddRef()
    {
      Interlocked.Increment(ref referenceCount);
    }

    public void Release()
    {
      if(Interlocked.Decrement(ref referenceCount) == 0)
      {
        refCountObject.Dispose();
      }
      return;
    }
  }
```

This essentially factors out all the reference-counting code from the **FileStreamRefCounted** class we first wrote in the previous reference counting section. In addition, it includes an **IDisposable** variable whose **Dispose( )** method will be called when the reference count drops to zero. A requirement is an **IDisposable** object must be passed to the constructor. Note also, the class is sealed and **CheckReferenceCount( )** is only called when **DEBUG** is defined (**cse.exe /D:DEBUG** ...) to maximize efficiency.

Now let's look at the **FileStreamRefCounted** class declaration:

```
namespace CSharpHeadStart
{
  using System;
  using System.IO;
  using ReferenceCounting;
  using System.Diagnostics;
```

```
public class FileStreamRefCounted : FileStream, IDisposable
  {

    public FileStreamRefCounted(string path, FileMode mode):
     base(path, mode)
     {
         RC = new IRefCountedImpl(this);
     }

    // Override other FileStream constructors here.

    // Just in case Dispose is not called explicitly
    // by the client.
    ~FileStreamRefCounted()
    {
      Dispose();
    }

    // **********
    // IDisposable
    public void Dispose()
    {
      this.Close();
      // Turn off the call to Finalize() by the GC.
      GC.SuppressFinalize(this);
      // Call base.Dispose() if implemented.
    }

    public RefCountedImpl RC;
  }
```

The key line is the last line. As you can see, *containment* essentially means adding what would normally be the parent class as a property to the containing class. Calling the reference counting methods requires the additional "RC" for the variable name, as in:

```
FileStreamRefCounted filestream;
...
filestream.RC.Release();
```

What does containment accomplish? First, it saves us from having to cut-and-paste the implementation code required for reference counting from one reference-counted class to another. This is important because now, if we need to change the **RefCountedImpl** class for some reason, there's only one place to make the change.

Avoiding duplicate code is arguably one of the most important features that multiple inheritance offers and containment offers a reasonable solution if this is all you need to accomplish.

What is the cost of using containment in place of multiple inheritance, however? As already pointed out, users of the class need to include the variable of the contained class whenever calling one of its methods or properties. This makes the methods and properties of the contained class a little more cumbersome to find but other than that, it is merely a slight inconvenience. More importantly, however, containment results in the loss of direct *substitutability* for the contained class. Substitutability is the characteristic of being able to pass the derived class (**FileStreamRefCounted**) as a parameter to any method or property that takes a data type of the parent class (or interface). In the example previous, **FileStreamRefCounted** cannot serve as a substitute to **IRefCounted** (or **RefCountedImpl**). For example, given the partial source for a new weak reference class, as the following shows, the constructor couldn't be passed to the **FileStreamRefCounted** object directly.

```
class WeakReferenceRefCounted : WeakReference
{
  WeakReferenceRefCounted(IRefCounted Target) :
    base(Target)
  {
    Target.AddRef()
  }
  ...
}


...
{
  FileStreamRefCounted filestream;
  WeakReferenceRefCounted(filestream);  // Error!!
...
}
```

Instead, **FileStreamRefCounted.RC** must be passed. A programmer could easily miss this, however, if the method used polymorphism such that **System.Object** was also supported because the program would still compile. In other words, if a **WeakReferenceRefCounted(System.Object)** constructor was provided, the previous code would compile, but would fail at run time. If substitutability is required, then an alternate solution is called for.

Interface Implementation

If substitutability is a requirement, then the alternative is to use multiple inheritance at the interface level and to code all the methods on the interface by hand. An implementation class (such as **RefCountedImpl**) is still helpful because it cuts down on the amount of cut-and-paste involved. Unlike the pure containment, however, the solution is more complicated than simply adding a field for the implementation class. A duplicate of all the methods and properties must be inserted into the class. Each of these methods would then have to call the methods of the implementation classes. Following is an implementation of **FileStreamRefCounted** using interface implementation. **RefCountedImpl** needs no changes.

```csharp
namespace CSharpHeadStart
{
  using System;
  using System.IO;
  using ReferenceCounting;
  using System.Diagnostics;

  public class FileStreamRefCounted :
    FileStream, IDisposable, IRefCounted
  {

    public FileStreamRefCounted(string Path, FileMode mode):
     base(Path, mode)
     {
         RC = new IRefCountedImpl(this);
     }
    // Override FileStream constructors here.

    // Just in case Dispose is not called explicitly
    // by the client.
    ~FileStreamRefCounted()
    {
      Dispose();
    }

    // **********
    // IDisposable
    public void Dispose()
    {
      this.Close();
      // Turn off the call to Finalize() by the GC.
      GC.SuppressFinalize(this);
```

```
      // Call base.Dispose() if implemented.
  }

  public RefCountedImpl RC;
  // **********
  // IRefCounted
  public void AddRef()
  {
    RC.AddRef();
  }
  public void Release()
  {
    RC.Release();
  }
}
```

This implementation of **FileStreamRefCounted** essentially has two differences. First, **FileStreamRefCounted** is derived from **IRefCounted**. This is what enables the substitutability. Given this inheritance, it's possible to use

```
WeakReferenceRefCounting wkrf =
  new WeakReferenceRefCounting( filestream );
```

in place of

```
WeakReferenceRefCounting wkrf =
  new WeakReferenceRefCounting( filestream.RC );
```

Because **IRefCounted** is added to the inheritance tree, however, the implementation also needs to be added. This is why the **AddRef( )** and **Release( )** methods have been added. Notice that what all these methods do is call the contained **RefCountedImpl** class stored in **RC**.

```
...
  RC.AddRef();
...
  RC.Release();
...
```

With interface inheritance, our class is a super set of the containment method previously mentioned. Interface inheritance provides the substitutability we were lacking in pure containment, however. What are the disadvantages? Essentially, that the methods and functions of implemented interface need to be added to the class. This is trivial when only two simple methods like those of **IRefCounted** exist, but more complicated interfaces could be troublesome. No doubt, once you have to implement five different methods (if not before), you'll resort to cutting-and-pasting the implementation code from one class to another. Furthermore, if a method in an inherited interface was added or changed (not recommended practice because it breaks the contract), then the method must be hand added or changed throughout all classes that implement the interface. Fortunately, a compile error results, but, nonetheless, the same change is required in multiple places. Solving this cut-and-paste problem requires macros, which we consider next.

Macros

As you learned in the previous chapter, C# doesn't support macros. A trivial workaround to this problem is to use the C++ preprocessor to expand the macros before running the C# compiler. To run only the C++ preprocessor, use the **/P** option. To forcefully include particular files, namely files that contain your macro definitions, use the **/FI** option. Finally, to compile the file as a CPP file, you also need the **/Tp** option. For the sample we've been working with, the command would be as follows:

```
cl.exe /P /Tp file.csm /FI RefCount.csm
```

Combining Macros with Interface Inheritance

The main problem with interface inheritance is the code required to implement the interfaced essentially becomes a cut-and-paste from class to class. One way to avoid this is to place all the code within a macro. In this scenario, you would add **REFCOUNTEDIMPL** to the class and define **REFCOUNTEDIMPL** as follows:

```
#define IREFCOUNTEDIMPL            \
  public IRefCountedImpl RC;       \
  public void AddRef()             \
  {                                \
    RC.AddRef();                   \
  }                                \
  public void Release()            \
  {                                \
    RC.Release();                  \
  }
```

This macro is inside **RefCount.csm**, where the **CSM** extension is added to indicate this is a C# macro file. You will notice from the preceding **cl.exe** command that this file is included in the compilation with the **/FI** option.

Given this macro file, improvising multiple inheritance essentially takes only three steps:

1. You have to add the interface to the list of parent classes. In our example, this involves adding **IRefCounted** (and **IDisposable**, if it isn't already there).

2. You need to include the macro within the class definition. Here's the final **FileStreamRefCounted** class definition in **File.csm**. REFCOUNTEDIMPL is all that's added.

```
public class FileStreamRefCounted :
  FileStream, IDisposable, IRefCounted
{

   // Override FileStream constructors here.

   // Just in case Dispose is not called explicitly
   // by the client.
   ~FileStreamRefCounted()
   {
     Dispose();
   }

   // ***********
   // IDisposable
   public void Dispose()
   {
     this.Close();
     // Turn off the call to Finalize() by the GC.
     GC.SuppressFinalize(this);
     // Call base.Dispose() if implemented.
   }

   // The macro below is used to pseudo implement multiple
   // inheritance
   REFCOUNTEDIMPL
   ...
}
```

3. You must add the additional compile step for executing the precompiler.

This last step can also be automated either via a make file, a batch file, or even a Visual Studio solution. Included in the source code, you will find a make file that can build the sample using macros automatically. Here is a listing of the file.

```
File.exe : File.i EntryPoint.cs
  csc.exe /D:DEBUG /R:System.dll /out:File.exe File.i \
    Refcount.cs EntryPoint.cs

File.i : File.csm RefCount.csm
  cl.exe /P /Tp file.csm /FI Refcount.csm
```

Given the make file, you can execute the build as follows:

```
nmake /f makefile
```

If you use a Visual Studio solution in place of the make file, you need to create an empty project that runs the precompile step, and then make your C# project dependent on the precompile project.

Templates

As we observed back in Chapter 4, another one of the features lacking in C# is templates. Unfortunately, the story for templates isn't as good as it was for macros and multiple inheritance (and these stories weren't exactly great). Two solutions exist.

The first solution is to use managed C++, which provides you with a limited set of template functionality. This is much more than is available with C#, however. It is limited because the template class cannot derive from a managed type and cannot be declared as a managed type. Essentially, you're limited to containment when it comes to a class template.

The second solution is to do without templates by using the **System.Object**. This solution involves replacing whatever data type would be specified in the template with **System.Object**. For example, consider the C++ template definition from Chapter 4, shown again in the following:

```
template <class T, class U>
struct Pair
{
  public Pair(T First, U Second)
  {
    this.First = First;
```

```
    this.Second = Second;
  }
  public T First;
  public U Second;
}
```

To implement a similar class in C#, where no templates exist, you need to use **System.Object** in place of **T** and **U**. A listing of the code follows:

```
struct Pair
{
  public Pair(System.Object First, System.Object Second)
  {
    this.First = First;
    this.Second = Second;
  }
  public System.Object First;
  public System.Object Second;
}
```

Or, you could code the class for the specific type you want, replacing **T** and **U** with the hard-coded types you need. In this case, you must create an entirely new class every time the pattern occurs, but for different data types. For example, if you were trying to pair a **Name** string to a **SSN** class, first you would be required to create a **PairNameSSN** class, whereas a **Team** class to **Coach** class pair would require an entirely different class, **PairTeamCoach**.

In the first case (using **System.Object**), the code isn't strongly typed such that it's possible to store an object of different types in the pair, even though this may not be what is desirable. If you were trying to pair a **Team class** to a **Coach class**, this would work, but there would be nothing to stop the programmer from placing the **Team** class in the **Second,** rather than **First** property, or vice versa. Templates are strongly typed such that this would be prevented (assuming the data types within the pair were different).

Neither of the previous design options achieves the same functionality that templates do, but they both present a reasonable workaround that C# programmers must live with until Microsoft adds generics to the CLR.

Another, slightly subtler drawback exists to using **System.Object**, which is all value types must be boxed when they are stored into the class. Later on, when it's time to remove the value types, an additional performance hit would be incurred to unbox the value.

Source Code Security

The last item that deserves mention in this chapter concerns the security of your code. Because IL is such an integral part of the .NET architecture, and because IL code is so easily available via utilities such as **ILDasm.exe**, the barrier to preventing users from stealing your source code by disassembling it is much smaller than it was previously. Prior to .NET (and Java), disassembling code was certainly possible, but the task was significantly more difficult than the one presented by IL code.

Some developers may not see this as much of a concern, but a few rather hair-raising scenarios could occur. Consider, for example, the malevolent user who disassembles your code, changes it to be malicious, and then redistributes the code. This could seriously impact a user's willingness to try the same application again. Certainly, certificates help this, but they require users to pay attention and to examine the certificates manually. Furthermore, authenticated certificates are rarely included in shareware/freeware products because of the added cost.

Another area that presents concern is an increased risk of piracy. Let's assume some location within your code checks for a license or verifies the maximum number of users of your distributed application hasn't been reached. Because IL code is so easy to disassemble and reassemble, what is to prevent a user from disassembling the code and removing any license checks you may have? Nothing is new about these possibilities in the .NET world; it's simply significantly easier to achieve now.

Complete solutions to this problem hadn't fully developed at press time. The most obvious solution would be to create some type of obfuscator that increases the complexity involved in interpreting what code does. At this time, Microsoft only claims it's aware and concerned about the problem, but it hasn't yet announced any solutions. If this issue is of great concern to you (for example, if you work on writing a messaging application for AOL and you don't want Microsoft to figure out how your application works), then the best solution is to write the portions of your application that require a lower level of visibility using an unmanaged language. The only alternative is to restrict your managed code to the server so that it is not accessible to prying eyes.

CHAPTER 6

Integrating Legacy Code with C#

IN THIS CHAPTER:

Integration Approaches

Calling COM Objects from C#

The COM Callable Wrapper, Calling .NET Objects from COM

Data Marshalling

Platform Invocation Services, Calling Unmanaged APIs from C#

Interoperability Through Managed C++

Migrating Code

Summary

C# and .NET are completely new platforms for development. However, plenty of Windows-based code already exists in the world, and most development staffs don't have the luxury of pitching what they've done and starting over. What this means is a critical feature of the .NET Framework is the capability to interoperate with existing, unmanaged code. Clearly, far more unmanaged code exists now than managed code. Any significant adoption of .NET as a development platform isn't practical without being able to easily integrate new managed code and existing unmanaged code. Fortunately, Microsoft realizes this and has provided a solid technical approach for integrating .NET with existing unmanaged code. This chapter describes the technologies available in .NET for integrating existing unmanaged code with .NET-managed code.

Integration Approaches

COM-based components are ubiquitous. In fact, most Windows-based services and add-ons have provided COM interfaces, hence, it's a given that existing COM-based components need to be integrated into .NET-based applications. The goals of .NET's COM interoperability features are to provide 100 percent compatibility with existing software. A standard COM client, for example, should have no idea it's talking to a .NET-managed object and a COM server should have no idea a .NET managed object is the COM client. In addition, a COM server upgraded to run in .NET should be capable of providing services to a COM client unchanged and, a client, upgraded to .NET, shouldn't be noticeable to a COM server.

One common integration scenario is an existing library of COM-based business objects that need to be deployed to the Web. ASP.NET is a vastly improved architecture for building and deploying Web-based applications and it can be leveraged without requiring the business objects to be rewritten. As depicted in Figure 6-1, the existing business objects can be used "as is" via the COM interoperability provided by .NET, while your new Web app leverages the updated services of ASP.NET.

Not only can existing COM be integrated easily into .NET, things work just as easily in the other direction. For example, consider an existing n-tier client/server application that uses Visual Basic (VB) as a front end. You want to start building .NET-based services, but you can't throw out the existing architecture and all the code that goes with it to start writing everything in C# for .NET. You can, however, start building new services that leverage the .NET Framework and expose them as COM objects for easy integration into your existing front end as shown in Figure 6-2.

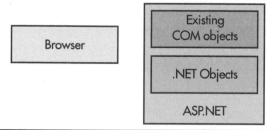

Figure 6-1   *ASP.NET hosting COM-based business objects*

Finally, if you have C++-based business components, these components can easily be added or accessed from your C++ application using Managed Extensions for C++. Managed Extensions can also be used to build .NET wrappers for your existing C++ classes to make them available to .NET-based applications. In fact, the primary reason Managed Extensions exist is to integrate existing C++ code into the managed world of .NET.

Calling COM Objects from C#

Having quickly reviewed some of the integration possibilities, we now delve into some of the mechanics of COM interoperability. First, we discuss the details of accessing COM components and then we look at interoperability using Managed C++. This detailed review of COM interoperability begins by importing a simple test COM component into .NET.

.NET supports both early binding (direct vtable calls) and late binding of COM-based components. To early bind, a managed class wrapper must be generated. If only **IDispatch** interfaces are available for the COM component, then late binding is required. Late binding from C# code requires the use of the .NET

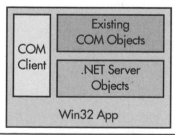

Figure 6-2   *Unmanaged client using .NET managed objects*

Reflection API. Remember from Chapter 4, VB.NET supports late binding natively. Also, remember language interoperability is a key feature of the .NET platform, so before you make a decision to implement Reflection API, consider using VB.NET to provide the wrapper if late binding is required.

Our first sample was built using the ATL Component Wizard of Microsoft Visual Studio 6.0. It represents nearly the simplest COM component that can be built. The IDL for the simple sample component can be found in **SampleSrv.idl** which is listed here:

```
import "oaidl.idl";
import "ocidl.idl";
   [
     object,
     uuid(9169E993-023A-43B3-B24D-73E34E64A6AE),
     dual,
     helpstring("IFirst Interface"),
     pointer_default(unique)
   ]
   interface IFirst : IDispatch
   {
     [id(1), helpstring("method Message")] HRESULT Message();
   };


[
   uuid(654E0999-0110-4D29-BFCE-4E8872943ECF),
   version(1.0),
   helpstring("SampleSrv 1.0 Type Library")
]
library SAMPLESRVLib
{
   importlib("stdole32.tlb");
   importlib("stdole2.tlb");

   [
     uuid(B3A9788C-FE73-426B-B2B7-0EB9C910ABC9),
     helpstring("First Class")
   ]
   coclass First
   {
```

```
    [default] interface IFirst;
  };
};
```

Using the TLBIMP Utility

To use the **SampleSrv** COM component from C#, managed types are required. The
.NET SDK provides the **TLBIMP.EXE** (**TLBIMP**) utility to generate .NET proxy
classes and associated metadata for COM libraries. The proxy classes are then used
by the .NET runtime to build a managed wrapper, called the Runtime Callable
Wrapper (RCW). The RCW wraps the COM component, so it can be called from
managed code, just as if it was a .NET managed type.

The following command line generates a .NET assembly from the simple COM
component **SampleSrv.dll**.

```
tlbimp SampleSrv.dll /out:SampleSrvAsm.dll
```

Running **ILDASM.EXE** on the generated assembly shows exactly what **TLBIMP**
does with the component and also provides a good idea of what's going on in the
RCW. The generated namespace is taken from the name of the assembly so, in
this case, it's **SampleSrvAsm**. Within this namespace, a class and an interface have
been generated corresponding to the **SampleSrv** declared interface **IFirst** and the
coclass First.

If, for some reason, the default namespace name isn't desirable, it can be
overridden with a specific custom attribute. Overriding the default name could be
appropriate if several related COM components are being imported, or if a naming
conflict needs to be avoided. The following line, placed into the IDL of the
SampleSrv library, gives it a namespace of **Sample.Test** instead of **SampleSrvAsm**
as shown in Figure 6-3.

```
custom(0F21F359-AB84-41e8-9A78-36D110E6D2F9, "Sample.Test")
```

TLBIMP also includes options to indicate or embed a key name into the
assembly. As with any assembly, a strong name can be supplied, so the .NET
security framework can be leveraged for this assembly and the .NET code can be
written to use it.

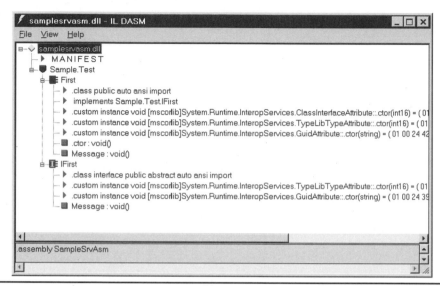

Figure 6-3   *SampleSrvAsm.DLL as viewed by ILDASM*

The Runtime Callable Wrapper

The RCW does just what its name implies: it provides a managed wrapper for COM objects so that they can be called by .NET managed types. Once an assembly for the COM library has been built, it's easily accessed inside the .NET Framework, just as if it were a standard assembly because of the efforts of the RCW. In fact, that's what the "outside" of the wrapper is—a .NET assembly. Inside the wrapper, COM objects are instantiated and manipulated for the purposes of the .NET client (see Figure 6-4).

The following sample code (located in **SampleClient.cs**) shows a simple C# program that uses our sample server. You won't notice anything special about this server. It uses the assembly by importing its namespace.

```csharp
using Sample.Test;

class EntryPoint
{
  public static void Main()
  {
    First f = new First();
    f.Message();
  }
}
```

That's all there is to it. As you can see, the RCW insulates the .NET managed world from the COM reference-counted world. The .NET clients shouldn't notice

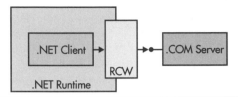

Figure 6-4   *The Runtime Callable Wrapper (RCW)*

anything unusual or even that they're using COM objects at all. The guts of the required COM interaction, including reference counting as well as converting data types, handling **HRESULTs**, return values, and wrapping connection points are all taken care of by the RCW.

In addition, the RCW, and underlying .NET marshaller, provide numerous standard type conversions. Most of these conversions are straightforward. The following reviews a few of the trickier or indirect conversions.

The convenience of the RCW doesn't come without a price. Every call from managed to unmanaged code bears some overhead. However, critical attention has been paid to performance of the RCW. Microsoft realizes the vast amount of existing COM-based code out there and it isn't enough just to make accessing it from .NET easy; it also has to perform when it gets called from .NET. The RCW is optimized so calls into COM provide minimal overhead (as few as ten machine instructions in cases where no marshalling is required).

Method Return Values and HRESULTs

One area where the RCW does some extra work is with method return values and **HRESULTs**. Notice, even though the **Message( )** method on the previous **First** object returned an **HRESULT**, it was converted to having void return in .NET. This is because the RCW maps .NET method return values to COM method **[out retval]** parameters. The **[retval]** parameter won't be included as a method parameter but, instead, determines the return type of the method and a method without a return value is declared as void.

The **HRESULT** isn't lost. When a COM server returns a failure **HRESULT**, the RCW generates a .NET exception that can then be handled using the .NET standard try, catch, finally mechanism. If the COM component supports the **ISupportErrorInfo** interface, the RCW will then make rich error information inside the .NET exception.

What this does mean, however, is success **HRESULTs** cannot be directly returned. To get success **HRESULTs** (Such as **S_FALSE** or **S_TRUE**) back from COM method calls, the **PreserveSigAttribute** is required and **TLBIMP** doesn't use this attribute by default. Therefore to get a nonfailure, **HRESULT** requires writing a custom callable wrapper.

COM Object Lifetime and Deterministic Finalization

The RCW COM objects are allocated from unmanaged memory, that is, they aren't managed by the .NET runtime. .NET doesn't add any features that change the basic responsibilities of the COM client to release references to the COM object. The RCW itself is garbage collected, however. To handle the COM referencing, the RCW maintains an internal cache to interface pointers and an RCW releases references to COM objects that it holds when the runtime garbage collector releases the RCW object. If the COM object needs to be released earlier, the explicit release mechanism is required and a call to the static method **Marshall.ReleaseComObject( )** does just that. If any further calls are made to the RCW that involve the wrapped object, an **InvalidComObjectException** will be generated.

Inheritance and RCW Objects

COM objects exposed to .NET as managed types through the RCW can be inherited just like any other managed type. A few caveats exist, however. To inherit from an RCW, the COM object it's wrapping must be early-bound, externally creatable, and COM-aggregatable.

Interface inheritance is also preserved with the exception of **IUnknown** and **IDispatch**. **IUnknown** and **IDispatch** are consumed (or called) by the RCW on an as-needed basis and aren't exposed through the managed RCW class. **IUnknown**'s **AddRef( )** and **Release( )** functionality is handled directly by the RCW. If necessary, **IDispatch** style interaction can be achieved via reflection.

COM Connection Points

The RCW also manages the conversion of COM connection point interfaces to C# events which is a considerable feature as these two approaches to implementing events are quite different. They are compatible enough that a conversion is possible, however.

To illustrate this conversion, we use a simple COM countdown timer component. This component implements a **Countdown** object that sources an **OnElapsedTimer( )** event. (This component comes straight from *COM+ Programming from the Ground Up* by Mark Michaelis (Osborne/McGraw-Hill)). The IDL for the event source is as follows:

```
[default, source] dispinterface _ICountdownEvents;
```

Note, the event source interface is prefixed with an underscore "_" so it's a hidden interface in environments like Visual Basic 6. This won't stop the interface from showing up in the generated metadata, however. When **TLBIMP** generates the metadata for the RCW, it generates a delegate named after the interface, followed by an underscore, and then followed by the name of the event. In the server, the name of the event is **OnTimeElapsedEventHandler( )**, therefore, the name of the delegate is **_ICountdownEvents_OnTimeElapsedEventHandler( )**.

To import the **Timers.DLL** into .NET, the following command line is used:

```
tlbimp Timers.dll /out:TimersAsm.dll
```

Once imported, the **TimersAsm.DLL** can be used like any other assembly. The following C# sample found in **CountdownClient**.cs shows the countdown timer in action.

```
// build command: csc CountdownClient.cs /r:TimersAsm.dll
using System;
using TimersAsm;

class EntryPoint
{
  static int TimerHandler(int RemainingIterations)
  {
    Console.WriteLine("Handled countdown timer");
    Console.WriteLine("  Remaining iterations: {0}",
      RemainingIterations);
  }

  public static void Main()
  {
    Countdown cd = new Countdown();
    // set the countdown interval
    cd.Interval = 2000;
    cd.IterationCount = 10;
    cd.OnTimeElapsed +=
      new _ICountdownEvents_OnTimeElapsedEventHandler(TimerHandler);

    string userInput;
    Console.WriteLine("Waiting for timers...");
    userInput = Console.ReadLine();
  }
}
```

In the previous code, the **TimersAsm** namespace generated by running **TLBIMP** on the **Timers.DLL** is used. Then, the event delegate method **TimerHandler( )** is declared. This method receives the **Countdown.OnTimerElapsed** event. Finally, an instance of **Countdown** is created and initialized, and a new delegate is created for the event handler.

Threading of the RCW Components

Developers who never got around to understanding the intricacies of each COM threading model or apartment type should be glad to know that, in .NET, the apartment architecture has essentially disappeared. This means all the complexities that accompanied these concepts have essentially evaporated and you needn't be concerned about them, unless you're still interfacing with COM components. The downside of no longer having the apartment model is now you, as the programmer, are responsible for your own synchronization in situations when concurrent threads could execute your code. We briefly touch on this in Chapter 3.

In the COM world, executables are required to initialize their threads as either single-threaded apartment or multithreaded apartment, using a call **CoInitializeEx(NULL, COINIT_APATMENTTHREADED)** or **CoInitializeEx(NULL, COINIT_MULTITHREADED)**, respectively. The need to do this when calling from the managed world into COM still exists, but rather than calling the Win32 API using **DLLImport**, you can set the apartment by changing the **ApartmentState** property of the current thread, as follows:

```
using System.Threading;
Thread.CurrentThread.ApartmentState = ApartmentState.STA;
TIMERSLib.Stopwatch stopwatch = new TIMERSLib.Stopwatch();
stopwatch.Interval = 10000;
```

Setting the **ApartmentState** to **ApartmentState.STA** initializes the apartment as a single-threaded apartment. To initialize the apartment as multithreaded, use **ApartmentState.MTA** or **ApartmentState.Unknown**.

If you neglect to initialize the state of an apartment then the CLR automatically initializes the apartment for you on the first call to a COM component. The default state in this case is **ApartmentState.MTA**. Therefore, you should initialize the apartment the thread runs in as soon as possible to ensure a compatible apartment with the component you're instantiating. If you fail to initialize the threading model, then the COM object may be instantiated into a different apartment, which would result in the marshalling of all calls to the COM object. Marshalling requires a proxy to be invoked, causing the performance to degrade.

As was true with COM, a thread cannot be changed from one apartment type to another. Therefore, setting the **ApartmentState** multiple times has no effect. Neither can the apartment state of the thread be uninitialized. In fact, there are times when the thread may have already been assigned an apartment (by a class you're accessing, for example) preventing you from initializing the apartment state yourself.

The COM Callable Wrapper, Calling .NET Objects from COM

As easily as .NET objects can use COM components, .NET objects themselves can be exposed as COM components. C# classes are exposed as COM objects using a COM Callable Wrapper (CCW).

As previously discussed, a likely reason to use a CCW is so you can develop new business objects using .NET, and then use these business objects from existing "legacy" applications. In this section, we rework our **HospitalEmployee** sample from Chapter 2, separating the patient monitor from the employee classes, and then building library assemblies. This helps us show the interoperability features in more consumable pieces. The user interface is a standard Win32-based application developed using Visual Basic 6.

The basic steps involved in getting an assembly exposed as COM objects are:

1. Build a .NET library assembly.

2. Export a type library from this assembly.

3. Register the assembly for use by COM clients.

4. Use the registered COM type library in an application.

Each of these steps is reviewed in more detail in the following.

We start by building and exporting an assembly with only the basic classes for hospital employees to keep things simple. First, look at the **HospitalEmployee** classes shown here:

```
// Build command: csc /t:library employees.cs
//
namespace HospitalEmployee
{
  using System;
```

```
public abstract class Employee
{
  private string name;
  public string Name
  {
    get { return name; }
    set { name = value; }
  }
}

public class Doctor : Employee
{
  public Doctor()
  {
  }
}

public class Nurse : Employee
{
  public Nurse()
  {
  }
}

}
```

This assembly is built using the following command:

```
csc /t:library employees.cs
```

TLBEXP Utility

Once we have our .NET assembly built, the **TLBEXP** utility is used to generate a COM-type library from a .NET assembly. The type library is then used by COM clients to call the .NET objects. Both early binding (direct vtable calls) and late binding (**IDispatch**) can be automatically generated, but only dispatch interfaces are generated by default. Because **IDispatch** is supported, your objects can be accessed from the Windows Scripting engine. One type library is generated per assembly.

The following command is used to generate the **Employees.tlb** file:

```
TLBEXP Employees.dll
```

Using the OLE/COM Viewer application included with Microsoft Visual Studio 6, the following IDL can be exported:

```
// Generated .IDL file (by the OLE/COM Object Viewer)
//
// typelib filename: <could not determine filename>

[
  uuid(4872AD93-E61B-3ABF-AA1B-4482E765885B),
  version(0.1)
]
library EmployeeS
{
    // TLib :
    // TLib : Common Language Runtime Library :
{BED7F4EA-1A96-11D2-8F08-00A0C9A6186D}
    importlib("mscorlib.tlb");
    // TLib : OLE Automation : {00020430-0000-0000-C000-000000000046}
    importlib("stdole2.tlb");

    // Forward declare all types defined in this typelib

    [
      uuid(1D607B80-34A4-33AD-8F47-2F4098779B59),
      version(1.0),
        custom({0F21F359-AB84-41E8-9A78-36D110E6D2F9},
"Hospital.Employee.Employee")
    ]
    coclass Employee {
        [default] interface IDispatch;
        interface _Object;
    };

    [
      uuid(5F1B8177-1A40-3DAC-B474-7F1547FCF316),
      version(1.0),
        custom({0F21F359-AB84-41E8-9A78-36D110E6D2F9},
          "Hospital.Employee.Doctor")
    ]
    coclass Doctor {
        [default] interface IDispatch;
        interface _Object;
    };
```

```
[
  uuid(ACA0E0E8-65CE-389E-8CD8-227BFFAA74B8),
  version(1.0),
    custom({0F21F359-AB84-41E8-9A78-36D110E6D2F9},
      "Hospital.Employee.Nurse")
]
coclass Nurse {
    [default] interface IDispatch;
    interface _Object;
};
};
```

Taking a closer look at the IDL illustrates some interesting aspects of how the CCW manages the conversion between COM and .NET. By default, a coclass is built for each of the public classes in the assembly. Pure **IDispatch** interfaces are exported, and there are no dispatch IDs and no custom interfaces other than to _Object. This is the default behavior to help bridge the gap between COM's strict component versioning rules and .NET's more flexible component versioning rules. The _Object interface represents .NET's System.Object. Inspecting the included mscorlib.tlb reveals _Object itself is a well-defined interface, which represents the public methods of **System.Object**.

```
[
  uuid(65074F7F-63C0-304E-AF0A-D51741CB4A8D),
  hidden,
  dual,
  nonextensible,
    custom({0F21F359-AB84-41E8-9A78-36D110E6D2F9}, "System.Object")
]
dispinterface _Object {
  properties:
  methods:
    [id(00000000), propget] BSTR ToString();
    [id(0x60020001)] VARIANT_BOOL Equals([in] VARIANT obj);
    [id(0x60020002)] long GetHashCode();
    [id(0x60020003)] _Type* GetType();
};
```

In this scenario, the COM clients are restricted to late binding, however, they're less likely to break as new versions of the .NET classes are exported.

To get direct vtable binding, or early binding, the default behavior can be directly overridden using the **ClassInterfaceAttribute** custom attributes. Three options are provided for the **ClassInterfaceAttribute**: **AutoDispatch**, **AutoDual**, and **None**. If no attribute is applied, **TLBEXP** acts as if **[ClassInterfaceAttribute(AutoDispatch)]** has been attached to all the exported classes. **[ClassInterfaceAttrubute(None)]** eliminates the IDispatch interface from the coclass, but retains the _Object interface. Finally, when **[ClassInterfaceAttrubute(AutoDual)]** is used, then a more complete interface is automatically generated. This is shown and then described in the following:

```
[ClassInterface(ClassInterfaceType.AutoDual)]
  public class Employee
{
  ...
}
```

First, an interface definition is automatically generated for the **Employee** class. The interface name is the public class name prefixed with an underscore, "_Employee". The **_Employee** interface is then used as a base interface for both the **Doctor** and **Nurse** implementation classes. This allows a client to ask the **Doctor** or **Nurse** specifically for its implemented **_Employee** interface. In addition, a closer look at the **_Employee** interface reveals the public members of the **Employee** class arc also exposed. This includes the derived public members of **System.Object**, as well as the implemented members of the **Employee** class. In our case, this is simply the **Name** property. The **Name** property itself is translated into COM property with **propput** and **propget** methods. The entire IDL is shown in the following:

```
// Generated .IDL file (by the OLE/COM Object Viewer)
// typelib filename: <could not determine filename>
[
  uuid(0C575428-3D34-3230-A484-248EFEF6B0F7),
  version(0.1)
]
library EmployeeS_CI
{
  // TLib : Common Language Runtime Library
  // : {BED7F4EA-1A96-11D2-8F08-00A0C9A6186D}
  importlib("mscorlib.tlb");
  // TLib : OLE Automation : {00020430-0000-0000-C000-000000000046}
  importlib("stdole2.tlb");

  // Forward declare all types defined in this typelib
```

```
interface _Employee;

[
  uuid(FD654229-861C-3FF3-A3CC-430F00B1AD52),
  version(1.0),
    custom({0F21F359-AB84-41E8-9A78-36D110E6D2F9},
"Hospital.Employee.Employee")
]
coclass Employee {
  [default] interface _Employee;
  interface _Object;
};

[
  uuid(A2841D87-68E5-37DA-8938-2628F2038FD4),
  version(1.0),
    custom({0F21F359-AB84-41E8-9A78-36D110E6D2F9}, "Hospital.Employee.Doctor")
]
coclass Doctor {
  [default] interface IDispatch;
  interface _Employee;
  interface _Object;
};

[
  uuid(B9858BCB-4866-3052-8523-D6234AC54C86),
  version(1.0),
    custom({0F21F359-AB84-41E8-9A78-36D110E6D2F9}, "Hospital.Employee.Nurse")
]
coclass Nurse {
  [default] interface IDispatch;
  interface _Employee;
  interface _Object;
};

[
  odl,
  uuid(316231A5-8A24-3CA1-B403-D1E8D8E036C3),
  hidden,
  dual,
  nonextensible,
```

```
      oleautomation,
        custom({0F21F359-AB84-41E8-9A78-36D110E6D2F9},
          "Hospital.Employee.Employee")
    ]
    interface _Employee : IDispatch {
      [id(00000000), propget]
      HRESULT ToString([out, retval] BSTR* pRetVal);
      [id(0x60020001)]
      HRESULT Equals(
        [in] VARIANT obj,
        [out, retval] VARIANT_BOOL* pRetVal);
      [id(0x60020002)]
      HRESULT GetHashCode([out, retval] long* pRetVal);
      [id(0x60020003)]
      HRESULT GetType([out, retval] _Type** pRetVal);
      [id(0x60020004), propget]
      HRESULT Name([out, retval] BSTR* pRetVal);
      [id(0x60020004), propput]
      HRESULT Name([in] BSTR pRetVal);
    };
};
```

Finally, notice **Doctor** and **Nurse** objects implement **IDispatch**, **_Employee**, and **_Object** but still don't expose their own public implementations. To expose their interfaces directly, the **[ClassInterface(ClassInterfaceType.AutoDual)]** also needs to be applied to their classes.

This approach, while it might require more work, also helps to enforce more careful planning on the part of the developer. Randomly emitting COM components is generally a bad thing because it leads inevitably to COM version nightmares. Well-defined interfaces that aren't likely to change can be defined explicitly, and then used as base interfaces for public classes. You can see this behavior in **System.Object** and the **_Object** interface. This interface isn't likely to change and, therefore, can be safely exposed to COM clients.

While a rich interface can be automatically exported using **[ClassInterface(ClassInterfaceType.AutoDual)]**, COM versioning issues should be carefully considered before deploying components this way. The recommended approach is to define and use interfaces. Interfaces are discussed further later in this chapter.

REGASM

COM clients cannot use the assembly and its type library until they're registered. .NET provides a special assembly registration utility—**REGASM**.exe (**REGASM**)—for this purpose. **REGASM** can also generate a TLB, just like **TLBEXP**, and it can optionally generate a .REG file to facilitate deployment of the component to other systems. The following command line can be used to register the Employees assembly, as well as to build a type library.

```
regasm /tlb:Employees.tlb /regfile:Employees.reg Employees.dll
```

Once the assembly is registered, it's ready to be used by COM clients. But first, please take note! One thing that many first-time "interoperators" miss, especially if they're used to COM library location, is it's the .NET runtime that loads the assembly, not COM. COM actually loads up MSCOREE.LIB when a client references your type library. This can quickly be verified by looking at the registry entries generated by **REGASM**.

```
[HKEY_CLASSES_ROOT\CLSID\{D83843D8-ACCE-3A29-B25F-14EEF5101AD0}\Inpro
cServer32]
@="C:\WINNT\System32\MSCorEE.dll"
"ThreadingModel"="Both"
"Class"="HospitalEmployee.Doctor"
"Assembly"="EmployeeS, Ver=0.0.0.0, Loc="""
```

What this means is standard .NET assembly location procedures are used to find your assembly, not simply the COM registry lookups. So, the COM client either must be in the same directory as the assembly, the assembly must be deployed to the Global Assembly Cache (GAC), or a custom configuration file is required. See Chapter 3 for additional details on how the CLR locates assemblies.

One final note on configuration before we move on: the "Assembly" item in the registry could be edited to include the path, but this isn't recommended for anything other than to facilitate testing during development. One of these entries is generated for each exported class and when the exact directory the assembly gets deployed to changes (which is likely), someone has to hack the registry. The .NET facilities provided are far more functional and easier to use once you understand them.

To use our newly exposed objects from Visual Basic, we simply add a reference and write some code against the interfaces. Nothing different or special is required. The following is a snippet of Visual Basic 6 code that uses the **Doctor** class. This sample code assumes a final version of **Employees.cs** in which the

AutoDualAttribute has also been applied to the **Doctor**. Without that attribute, late binding must be used.

```
Dim d As New Doctor
d.Name = Text1.Text
MsgBox "Hello Dr. " & d.Name
```

COM Callable Wrapper

The set of features and functions the .NET runtime loads to interact with a COM object is called the COM Callable Wrapper, or CCW. The CCW does exactly what its name implies: it wraps your .NET types in such a way that COM can be called on them. The CCW is a proxy that allows COM calls to cross from unmanaged to managed code, managing COM reference-counting and marshalling data as required. One CCW is created for each .NET object and, as previously discussed, your classes aren't invoked directly by the COM client. Instead, the core .NET runtime is invoked and, with it, the CCW, which is then responsible for loading and invoking instances of your classes. The .NET core runtime implements the COM interfaces for the COM clients. See Figure 6-5.

The .NET core runtime also implements **IUnknown** for reference counting and **IDispatch** for late binding to your .NET objects. These interfaces aren't seen or required by the .NET object. The CCW itself isn't a managed object. It maintains its own memory separate from the .NET managed world, so it can interoperate properly with the unmanaged world.

Additional interfaces are constructed or synthesized on demand by the CCW. These are COM interfaces useful to clients you don't have to worry about implementing. This includes **IDispatch**, **IProvideClassInfo**, **ISupportErrorInfo**, **IErrorInfo**, **IConnectionPoint** and **IConnectionPointContainer**, and **IObjectSafety**.

The CCW itself is not garbage collected, but the .NET objects it wraps are. The CCW maintains its own heap and is reference-counted. When COM clients release all references to the .NET object the CCW wraps, it removes itself from memory,

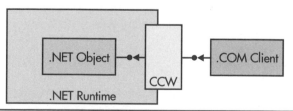

Figure 6-5   *COM Callable Wrapper (CCW)*

thereby releasing the reference to the managed object it was wrapping. Only at this point will the garbage collector be able to clean up the memory from these resources.

Interfaces

Before we continue on to the next topic that covers exposing .NET Events to COM Clients, let's spend a few minutes discussing COM interfaces and versioning.

As you saw previously in this section, all public methods on a class are exported when AutoDual is specified. This includes derived objects that are flattened in the default hierarchy. If you don't want all your exported objects to have the **System.Object** methods, you can override this behavior by defining an interface for the class. In this way, you can determine exactly what's exposed from your class.

The following source is used in the next section on events, but for purposes of our discussion here, the focus is on the class definition and the **IPatient** interface.

The following interface is defined for **IPatient**:

```
public interface IPatient
{
  string Name
  {
    get;
    set;
  }
  event MonitorDelegate HandleMonitorEvent;
  void FireMonitorEvent(bool IsEmergency);
}
```

Then, that interface is used to derive the **PatientMonitor** class as follows:

```
public class PatientMonitor : IPatient
{
  ...
}
```

IPatient is then listed as an interface on the class. Multiple interfaces can be inherited in this way. Note, **TLBEXP** adds some interfaces on its own, most notably **_Object**.

PatientMonitor uses **IPatient** to control what the external COM client sees for the class. Changes to the public interface of **PatientMonitor** for managed types won't be exposed automatically to COM. This helps keep the COM interfaces immutable. When the interface does need to change, **IPatient** is then updated and a new interface ID (IID) is generated, indicating a new version of the interface is now available. To preserve the old interface, a new interface could also be derived from **IPatient** and exposed.

Once **IPatient** is defined, the default **_Patient** generated by **AutoDual** is no longer required. This results in a class that's significantly less cluttered and easier to use than the default.

Providing .NET Events to COM Clients

If the .NET types you expose to COM fire events, it's highly likely you'll want your COM clients to be able to register for and receive these events. COM clients can use the events in one of two ways: first, the COM client can implement the delegate interface exposed by your type library directly and, second, the .NET type can be tagged with a custom attribute that **TLBEXP** uses to define a source event interface so the events are exposed as standard COM-connection point style events.

To show events, we use a modified version of the **PatientMonitor** class from Chapter 2. We also use the lessons previously learned about interfaces and define a default interface for the **PatientMonitor** class called **IPatient**. This restricts the public members of **PatientMonitor** to those defined by **IPatient**.

```
namespace Hospital.Interfaces
{
  using System;
  using System.Runtime.InteropServices;

  public delegate void MonitorDelegate(bool IsEmergency);

  public interface IPatient
  {
    string Name
    {
      get;
      set;
    }
    event MonitorDelegate HandleMonitorEvent;
    void FireMonitorEvent(bool IsEmergency);
  }
}

namespace Sample
{
```

```csharp
using System;
using System.Timers;
using Hospital.Interfaces;

public class PatientMonitor : IPatient
{
  public PatientMonitor()
  {
    // Fire up the monitor as soon as we're created.
    StartMonitorTimer();
  }

  // Our public event monitor
  public event MonitorDelegate HandleMonitorEvent;

  // private value that indicates
  // an emergency situation
  private bool emergencyFlag;
  // store the name of the patient we're monitoring
  private string patientName;

  /// An internal timer is used to simulate
  /// monitor events
  /// In our demo, the monitor goes off every 2 seconds
  /// and alternates between a normal call or an
  /// emergency call
  private void StartMonitorTimer()
  {
    Timer sleepTimer = new Timer();
    sleepTimer.Tick += new EventHandler(OnTimedEvent);
    sleepTimer.Interval = 2000;
    sleepTimer.Enabled =true;
  }

  /// When the timer Tick event is raised, we fire our monitor event
  void OnTimedEvent(object source, EventArgs e)
  {
    // Indicate whether this is an emergency
    FireMonitorEvent(emergencyFlag);
    emergencyFlag = !emergencyFlag;
  }

  // FireMonitorEvent fires event delegates if
```

```
    // there are any.
    public void FireMonitorEvent(bool IsEmergency)
    {
      Console.WriteLine("Monitor Event!");
      if(HandleMonitorEvent != null)
      {
        // Use the private delegate instance to invoke
        // the delegate methods
        HandleMonitorEvent(IsEmergency);
      }
    }

    public string Name
    {
      get
      {
        return patientName;
      }
      set
      {
        patientName = value;
      }
    }
  }
}
```

By default (with no interoperability attributes applied), **TLBEXP** generates **add_HandleMonitorEvent** and **remove_MonitorEvent** methods that take an **IDispatch** pointer. A client can then implement a compliant class and pass the **IDispatch** pointer to add or remove itself from the events. The following IDL was generated by compiling **PatientMonitor.cs** into an assembly, and then using the OLEView utility to save the generated IDL.

```
// Generated .IDL file (by the OLE/COM Object Viewer)
//
// typelib filename: PatientMonitor.tlb

[
  uuid(65F0C790-7B4B-3431-9FBB-E5385729632C),
  version(0.1)
]
library PatientMonitor
```

```
{
  // TLib :
  // TLib : Common Language Runtime Library
  // : {BED7F4EA-1A96-11D2-8F08-00A0C9A6186D}
  importlib("mscorlib.tlb");
  // TLib : OLE Automation : {00020430-0000-0000-C000-000000000046}
  importlib("stdole2.tlb");

  // Forward declare all types defined in this typelib
  interface IPatient;

  [
    uuid(39F079AA-E1C7-3110-885B-7CC60C3D0F59),
    version(1.0),
    noncreatable,
      custom({0F21F359-AB84-41E8-9A78-36D110E6D2F9},
        "Hospital.Interfaces.MonitorDelegate")
  ]
  coclass MonitorDelegate {
    [default] interface IDispatch;
    interface _Delegate;
    interface _Object;
    interface ICloneable;
    interface ISerializable;
  };

  [
    odl,
    uuid(FACCC94A-6AF8-3E7B-B2E6-E624FE293167),
    version(1.0),
    dual,
    oleautomation,
      custom({0F21F359-AB84-41E8-9A78-36D110E6D2F9},
        "Hospital.Interfaces.IPatient")
  ]
  interface IPatient : IDispatch {
    [id(0x60020000), propget]
    HRESULT Name([out, retval] BSTR* pRetVal);
    [id(0x60020000), propput]
    HRESULT Name([in] BSTR pRetVal);
    [id(0x60020002)]
    HRESULT add_HandleMonitorEvent([in] IDispatch* value);
    [id(0x60020003)]
```

```
    HRESULT remove_HandleMonitorEvent([in] IDispatch* value);
    [id(0x60020004)]
    HRESULT FireMonitorEvent([in] VARIANT_BOOL IsEmergency);
  };

  [
    uuid(3E6AEB36-FAF4-31FA-8EA9-C737606F233F),
    version(1.0),
      custom({0F21F359-AB84-41E8-9A78-36D110E6D2F9}, "Sample.PatientMonitor")
  ]
  coclass PatientMonitor {
    [default] interface IDispatch;
    interface _Object;
    interface IPatient;
  };
};
```

While what's provided by default is okay, it's not quite what we're looking
for in terms of event integration. Luckily, it's also not the final answer. We
can add connection-point style interfaces with the addition of the
ComSourceInterfacesAttribute( ) to the **PatientMonitor** class. When **TLBEXP**
sees this, it generates appropriate interface definitions and, when the CCW loads the
object, it performs the appropriate event marshalling. Note, this also requires us to
define an interface for the event, which is the recommended approach anyway. In
this way, the COM clients have a well-defined interface to support, even if they
decide not to use connection points.

Here are the additions to the PatientMonitor:

```
[InterfaceTypeAttribute(ComInterfaceType.InterfaceIsIUnknown)]
public interface IMonitorEvent
{
  void HandleMonitorEvent(bool IsEmergency);
}


...
[ComSourceInterfaces("Hospital.IMonitorEvent")]
public class PatientMonitor : IPatient
{
  ...
}
...
```

These source additions cause corresponding changes to the generated type library. Note, the following includes only the new lines of IDL. First, a new interface is defined for **IMonitorEvent**:

```
[
  odl,
  uuid(FF624E40-C849-3AB9-A792-202E1A76B6E5),
  version(1.0),
  oleautomation,
    custom({0F21F359-AB84-41E8-9A78-36D110E6D2F9},
      "Hospital.Interfaces.IMonitorEvent")
]
interface IMonitorEvent : IUnknown {
  HRESULT _stdcall HandleMonitorEvent([in] VARIANT_BOOL IsEmergency);
};
```

The **IMonitorEvent** is included in the **PatientMonitor** coclass and is tagged as the default event source.

```
[default, source] interface IMonitorEvent;
```

This enables COM clients to use the event as they would any other. The sample code includes a **PatientMonitor** Visual Basic application that uses the events.

Supporting IDispatch-based Events

To use events from a scripting environment or any environment that doesn't support dual interfaces, you also need to use **IDispatch** style events. To tag the event interface as a **dispinterface**, another interface is defined with the **InterfaceTypeAttribute** but, this time, **InterfaceIsIDispatch** is specified.

```
[InterfaceTypeAttribute(ComInterfaceType.InterfaceIsIDispatch)]
public interface IDispMonitorEvent
{
  void HandleMonitorEvent(bool IsEmergency);
}
```

To support both dual and dispatch-only environments, two interfaces must be defined: one for the standard dual interface and one for **IDispatch**. Multiple interfaces can be specified in the **ComSourceInterfaceAttribute** by separating the interfaces with a null, which the following demonstrates:

```
[ComSourceInterfaces(
"Sample.Interfaces.IMonitorEvent\0Sample.Interfaces.IDispMonitorEvent"
)]
public class PatientMonitor : IPatient
{
  ...
}
```

If dispatch interfaces are used, remember, the server is now calling late bound into the dispatch-based client. Therefore, the invocation of the event delegate for a dispatch-based interface cannot be done directly, but must be done using reflection.

Threading of .NET Components

In COM, an object indicates which apartment it can run in by a setting in the registry. Some COM objects can run in any apartment, while others can only run in an STA, MTA, or, if on Windows 2000+, a Thread Neutral apartment. All classes in .NET are assigned the "Both" threading model. Therefore, managed classes instantiated by COM are instantiated into the same apartment as the calling apartment. By assigning managed classes to be the threading model "both", you can avoid having calls go through a proxy when invoking a method on the managed class. The only time a proxy is required, therefore, is when the managed class is passed to a COM object that's running in a different apartment.

Additional COM Interoperability Attributes

We already mentioned several COM interoperability attributes in this section. .NET provides several additional attributes that can be used to control the actions of the CCW. The more relevant of these are discussed in this section.

Controlling GUIDs and Dispatch IDs

The **GuidAttribute( )** is used to assign a GUID explicitly to a class. If the GUID isn't explicitly assigned, then a GUID is automatically generated at export time. The value of the GUID is generated from a hash that includes the fully qualified class name, which guarantees both uniqueness, as well as that it will be the same every time it's generated, as long as the class definition doesn't change. Explicitly assigning this GUID via the **GuidAttribute( )** would allow the same GUID to be used across changes. This is most appropriate during development because using the same GUID for different implementations is against standard COM guidelines. Here is an example of how to use the **GuidAttribute( )**.

```
[GuidAttribute("7BE8FAD1-BDB7-437d-AAA2-E92705518800")]
public class Test
{
}
```

Managed interface declarations are exported as COM interfaces. The IID of the interface is automatically generated if it isn't supplied by the managed declaration. The IID is generated from a hash of the fully-qualified interface name as well as each method signature on the interface. Therefore, a change in the method signatures results in a new IID. The **GuidAttribute( )** can also be used to set the IID just as it was for the class.

Class Visibility

The **ComVisibleAttribute( )** can be used to hide or show types from COM that would otherwise be public. Applied at the interface or class level, **ComVisibleAttribute( )** hides a managed type from COM or explicitly makes the class available to COM. The attribute can also be applied to an entire assembly, which then enables you to select explicitly which public .NET types to make visible.

Default ProgID

The default COM ProgID is the namespace followed by the class name. The **ProgIdAttribute** can be used to override this behavior and explicitly provide the class name.

Additional .NET to Type Library Conversions

When a type library is generated from a .NET assembly, some additional conversions take place beyond what was discussed already in this section. The following discusses some of the more significant conversions.

Translating HRESULTs and Method Return Values

In reverse fashion to the RCW, the CCW translates .NET server object exceptions into failure **HRESULTs**. Exceptions include an **HRESULT** property for this very reason and, therefore, any custom exception you define should also initialize **HRESULT** in its constructor.

As exceptions are translated to **HRESULT**s, so, too, are return values translated to **[out, retval]** parameters. When success-based **HRESULT**s are required, the **PreserveSigAttribute( )** can be used to tell the CCW not to perform the typical translation.

Type Library Version

Version information in the type library is two digits, while it's four digits in a .NET assembly. The first two parts of the assembly version are kept and the last two are lost. However, if no version is specified, as in our sample, the default version in the .NET assembly is 0.0.0.0, which converts to 0.1 in the typelib.

```
[
  uuid(64F572ED-D8EB-39C8-96D7-745F38AC68B3),
  version(0.1)
]
```

Duplicate Type Names

Type names are generally exported as they're named in the C# type definition, but without the namespace to qualify it. This may lead to a collision in a large namespace. If it does, the **TLBEXP** numbers the second class name with an underscore ("_") and a number. For the first duplicate it finds, it uses the number 2. In our sample, we defined a **Hospital.Interfaces** namespace and we added a **Hospital.Utilities** namespace. If we add a class **Test** to both of them, the second one will be named **Test_2** when it's exported.

Enum Type Conversion

Enum types are exported as COM enum types, with each of the enum members prefixed with the enum name to insure uniqueness. The sample enum from Chapter 2, is exported as follows:

```
typedef [uuid(C8E957A3-952E-33A2-A71F-838C40C9A53C)       ,
custom({0F21F359-AB84-41E8-9A78-36D110E6D2F9},
"Sample.Utilities.TheWays")]
enum {
  TheWays_North = 1,
  TheWays_South = 2,
  TheWays_East = 3,
  TheWays_West = 4
} TheWays;
```

Data Marshalling

The .NET runtime provides a rich, optimized data marshaller for transferring data types between managed and unmanaged code. The same data marshalling engine is used by both .NET's COM and Platform Invoke (PInvoke) services (to be described shortly). Most data marshalling is straightforward, but a few caveats and special cases should be discussed.

The marshaller recognizes isomorphic types that don't require any conversion because they have identical representations in both managed and unmanaged code. *Isomorphic types* include all integer and real data types, as well as pointers to functions.

Nonisomorphic types are those that may require some conversion between managed and unmanaged code. The conversion may vary based on the situation. Let's look at Boolean type marshalling as an example. When Boolean is marshaled for the purpose of PInvoke, the type is converted to a 2-byte value, with true being represented by 1 and false by 0. When Boolean is marshaled for COM interoperability, it is to the COM VARIANT_BOOL type: true is –1, and false is 0. Another example is char, which is converted to either an ANSI or a Unicode character.

Parameters may be marked with the **InAttribute( )** and/or **OutAttribute( )**, which can provide some useful information to the marshaller and can reduce expensive data marshalling. In particular, the marshaller may decide it only has to do the conversion in a single direction. In the absence of the attribute, the marshaller assumes all parameters are In/Out.

Strings and the MarshalAsAttribute

If something beyond a standard conversion is required, **MarshalAsAttribute( )** can be used to provide some control over data marshalling. To illustrate the attribute, let's look at the default string behavior, and then see how it can be changed with **MarshalAsAttribute( )**.

The default behavior for a string conversion in the COM case is to use the COM BSTR type as the following illustrates.

```
public void Test2(string TestMessage)
```

This yields IDL, as follows:

```
HRESULT Test2([in] BSTR TestMessage);
```

If we want to be sure to expose a plain wide character string for Unicode purposes, it can be specified as follows:

```
public void Test2([MarshalAs(UnmanagedType.LPWStr)] string TestMessage)
```

Which yields the following IDL:

```
HRESULT Test2([in] LPWSTR TestMessage);
```

Marshalling Objects

In addition to all the native and string-type marshalling available, standard and default marshalling is also provided for objects.

A common occurrence for an object library is to return a reference of one type or another to a client. In the following sample code, we define an **EmployeeFactory** class, which is derived from **IEmployeeFactory** interface. The **EmployeeFactory** defines a method for returning an employee object to the client.

```
public interface IEmployeeFactory
{
   Employee GetEmployee(string Name);
}

public class EmployeeFactory : IEmployeeFactory
{
   public Employee GetEmployee(string Name)
   {
     // code to find and return employee
     // goes here
   }
}
```

By default, the following interface is generated:

```
interface IEmployeeFactory : IDispatch {
  [id(0x60020000)]
  HRESULT GetEmployee(
    [in] BSTR Name,
    [out, retval] IDispatch** pRetVal);
};
```

We can see **GetEmployee( )** returns an **IDispatch** pointer by default. If we use an interface to define the **Employee** object, then a tighter binding will be seen in this method. When **ClassInterfaceAttribute** is applied to the **Employee** class using the **AutoDual** option, we get the following result:

```
interface IEmployeeFactory : IDispatch {
  [id(0x60020000)]
  HRESULT GetEmployee(
    [in] BSTR Name,
    [out, retval] _Employee** pRetVal);
};
```

The previous example used the **_Employee** interface to return an object reference to the user. This is not always desired. In some cases, late binding may be preferred, especially if different types of employees have different methods. If the **GetEmployee( )** method is defined as returning an object, then it will be marshaled across the COM boundary as a **VARIANT*** by default. Additional **MarshallAs( )** attributes exist to control the conversion from object if either an **IDispatch** or even **IUnknown** is desired. First, let's consider the default behavior. If we change the **GetEmployee( )** method as defined on the **IEmployeeFactory** interface to return object instead of Employee as follows:

```
public object GetEmployee(string Name)
```

the following IDL will be generated.

```
HRESULT GetEmployee([in] BSTR Name, [out, retval] VARIANT* pRetVal);
```

MarshallAsAttribute( ) can be used to override that behavior. If the method is defined as follows

```
[return:MarshalAs(UnmanagedType.IUnknown)]
 object GetEmployee(string Name)
```

it yields the following IDL:

```
HRESULT GetEmployee([in] BSTR Name,
   [out, retval] IUnknown** pRetVal);
```

Finally, if, in spite of the interface just defined, **IDispatch** is still desired, the following method declaration

```
[return:MarshalAs(UnmanagedType.IDispatch)]
object GetEmployee(string Name);
```

yields the following IDL:

```
HRESULT GetEmployee([in] BSTR Name,
  [out, retval] IDispatch** pRetVal);
```

These are only some of the conversions provided. The Platform SDK includes specifications for both Data Marshalling and COM Interoperability, in which many additional details are covered. The COM Interoperability Specification includes two appendixes that detail the default type export and import conversions.

Finally, if the provided conversions aren't enough, custom wrappers can be constructed.

Platform Invocation Services, Calling Unmanaged APIs from C#

The .NET Framework also includes support for directly calling unmanaged APIs provided by DLLs. This is referred to as Platform Invocation, or PInvoke for short.

PInvoke services include handling exceptions and raising them in the client. These services also insure that any class—as well as any client to the class making the PInvoke calls—is fully trusted.

We begin with the "Hello World" of PInvoke applications, which is calling the Win32 **MessageBox( )** API. This is a simple API and can actually come in handy when you need to pop up a message. (Note, this functionality is supported in both the WinForms and VisualBasic namespaces, too.) Win32 APIs and any DLL-based public function can be accessed directly from within C# using the **DLLImportAttribute( )** as the following illustrates.

```
public class Utilities
{
  [DllImport("user32.dll")]
  public static extern int MessageBox(int hWnd, string Text,
    string Caption, uint Type);
}
```

This can be called from code as follows:

```
Utilities.MessageBox(0, "hello there", "C# Developer's Headstart", 0);
```

The next sample uses the Win32 API **GetComputerName( )** to return the current computer name into the supplied buffer. The Windows API declaration for GetComputerName looks like this:

```
BOOL GetComputerName(
  LPTSTR lpBuffer,   // computer name
  LPDWORD lpnSize    // size of name buffer
);
```

Note, **StringBuilder** is used so we can easily initialize a string buffer of a predetermined size. Also, because the second parameter of the API calls for a pointer to a DWORD, we need to insure that our call is by reference, so the **ref** keyword is used in the declaration, as well as in the call. The C# declaration for this function and the method that uses it look like this:

```
[DllImport("kernel32.dll", EntryPoint="GetComputerName")]
public static extern int GetComputerNameAPI(
  StringBuilder Buffer, ref int Size);

public static string GetComputerName()
{
  int sizeBuffer = 80;
  StringBuilder nameBuffer = new StringBuilder(sizeBuffer);
  int result = GetComputerNameAPI(nameBuffer, ref sizeBuffer);
  return nameBuffer.ToString();
}
```

Note, we use the **EntryPoint** setting on the DllImport attribute to change the name of the function, so we can add our own **GetComputerName( )** method directly to our **Utility** class.

API functions that require callbacks may also be invoked using delegates. Clearly, calling directly into the .NET managed environment isn't valid, so PInvoke marshals the delegate to a function pointer that's appropriate for receiving the callback, and then invokes the delegate from the function.

Interoperability Through Managed C++

Possibly one of the easiest ways to interoperate between the managed and unmanaged world—at least for C++ programmers—is to use Managed C++. If you have an existing C++ application, then adding Managed C++ code to that provides a great means of exposing it to the managed world. Furthermore, through Managed C++, you can easily access the abundance of classes within the .NET Framework along with any additional classes you may write in the managed world. Weaving Managed C++ among unmanaged C++ provides a great means for intertwining both the managed and the unmanaged world together within one language without the need to use **TLBIMP** or **TLBEXP** and COM. If you're trying to access numerous Win32 API, (not made available through the .NET Framework) and you don't want to go through PInvoke for each method you're calling—as you would in your C#—then using unmanaged C++ to make the API calls and Managed C++ to provide the interface is a convenient solution.

In this section, we briefly introduce Managed C++ and discuss the various options it provides for interoperability. This section is targeted at existing C++ programmers and isn't intended to be a complete Managed C++ reference. Instead, this is intended to be a survey, so you can understand how Managed C++ can be used as an interoperability solution.

Adding Managed C++ code to native C++ has two steps. The first is to use the **cl.exe** compiler (the C/C++ compiler) with the **/CLR** option. This option causes the compiler to insert managed code into the executable. If you run Managed C++ code through the debugger, you'll notice, just as with C#, the first instruction is a jump instruction to the MSCOREE library. In other words, the CLR gets loaded immediately and, essentially, takes control of the process, appropriately calling into the managed and unmanaged worlds as required.

NOTE

*To compile your C++ code for the Common Language Runtime, use the **/CLR** switch. This provides access to the Managed C++ extensions. At a minimum, all projects are required to have #using <mscorlib.dll> defined.*

The next step is to use the new preprocessor command **#using**, which adds a reference to a project in a similar fashion to the **/r:<assembly>** option found in the

C# compiler, **csc.exe**. At a minimum, all projects are required to have **#using <mscorlib.dll>** defined. The following is a variation on hello world. (Note, the **/MD** option is required for linking to the **MSVCRT.LIB**.)

```
//Build command: cl.exe /GX ByeBye.cpp /CLR /MD
//Debug build command cl.exe /Zi /GX ByeBye.cpp /CLR /MDd
#using <mscorlib.dll>
#include <iostream>
using namespace std;
void main()
{
  std::cout << "Bye bye, boys! Have fun storming the castle!\n";
  System::Console::WriteLine("Think it will work?");
  std::cout << "It would take a miracle.\n";
}
```

In this sample (**ByeBye.cpp**), notice the use of STL's (Standard Template Library) **cout** class to write to standard out. Immediately following, is the .NET Framework method for the same function, **System::Console::WriteLine( )**. Notice standard C++ syntax is used in the call to the .NET Framework. For example, in place of the "dot" operator, the namespace operator of two colons is used. The same operator is used for calling the static method **WriteLine( )**. Managed C++ conforms to native C++ syntax, although some additional keywords have been added, as you will see shortly.

If you use Managed C++ classes within your code, the same rules for garbage collection apply as those that accompany all managed types. Therefore, even though you use **new** to instantiate your classes, you needn't code in a call to **delete**. To do so isn't an error; it simply isn't necessary because the garbage collector is responsible for cleaning up your classes if you don't. The following is some sample code (**WebDump.cpp**) that demonstrates the principal.

```
//Build command: cl.exe /GX file.cpp /CLR
//Debug build command cl /Zi /GX file.cpp /CLR

#include <iostream>
using namespace std;

#using <mscorlib.dll>
using namespace System;
```

```
#using <System.Net.dll>
using namespace System::Net;
using namespace System::IO;

void main()
{
  String* URL;
  Stream* stream;
  int bytes_read = 0;
  int total_bytes_read = 0;
  const int max_to_read = 255;
  Byte buffer[] = new Byte[max_to_read];

  Console::WriteLine("Enter the URL (http://<domain>/...):");
  URL = Console::ReadLine();

  WebRequest* myRequest =
    WebRequestFactory::Create("http://localhost/localstart.asp");

  stream = myRequest->GetResponse()->GetResponseStream();

  while((bytes_read = stream->Read(buffer, 0, max_to_read)))
  {
    total_bytes_read+=bytes_read;
    Console::WriteLine(Text::Encoding::ASCII->GetString(buffer));
  }
  return;
}
```

In the previous code, the static method **WebRequestFactory::Create( )** returns an instantiated **WebRequest** class. You'd normally have to call **delete** in standard C++ (or **Release( )** for COM). In this case, however, **delete** isn't called explicitly and, instead, we rely on the garbage collector to clean up any instantiated managed classes. The one advantage of calling **delete** is it invokes an immediate call into your **destructor**, rather than waiting for the garbage collector to handle this for you. Note, just as with C#, a destructor in your managed class is converted to an IL **Finalize( )** method by the compiler.

In C++, all managed class variables are declared as pointers:

```
String* URL;
Stream* stream;
Byte buffer[] = new Byte[max_to_read];
...
```

Furthermore, notice that to avoid using the fully qualified name, such as **System::String**, you can bring a class into the global namespace using the standard C++ syntax, **using namespace**.

The previous code demonstrates how easy calling the .NET Framework is from your C++ code by adding the **/CLR** option and the **#using <mscorlib.dll>** preprocessor command. The other obvious scenario, however, is calling your C++ code from within the managed world. The answer is partly the same. However, you also need to create managed types within your C++ code. This generates IL code, just as any C# or VB class does. Through Managed C++, you can include C++ in the list of languages that interoperate on the .NET platform.

To write Managed C++, you need to use some of the managed extensions for C++. The managed extensions are new custom compiler directives that cause the compiler to generate IL code in place of assembler code. For example, to declare a C++ class as a managed class, you decorate the class with the **__gc** managed extension, as shown in this code snippet from **WhoAmI.cpp**:

```
// Build Command:
// Module: cl.exe WhoAmI.cpp /CLR:noAssembly /LD /link advapi32.lib
//   (Use this if calling from C#.)

#using <mscorlib.dll>

#include <windows.h>
#include <lmcons.h>  // Includes definition of UNLEN.

__gc class CCurrentUser
{
public:
  __property System::String* get_Name()
  {
    WORD length=UNLEN;
    TCHAR m_username[UNLEN + 1];
    GetUserName((LPTSTR)&m_username, (LPDWORD)&length);
    return m_username;
  }
};
```

This class can be used within your C++ code or from C# (or any .NET language). To access the class from C#, you need to include a reference to the class. The following is the C# code used to access the class.

```
// Build Command:
// csc.exe /addmodule:WhoAmI.dll WhoAmI.cs
// Note: Be sure to compile WhoAmI.cpp first.

namespace CSharpHeadStart
{
  class EntryPoint
  {
    static void Main()
    {
      CCurrentUser me = new CCurrentUser();
      System.Console.WriteLine(me.Name);
      return;
    }
  }
}
```

You can also declare value types in your Managed C++ code using the **__value** keyword. Although the **struct** keyword is used with this declaration, this is simply to be consistent with C#'s way of declaring value types. **Class** could also be used with the value type declaration, if so desired, because memory management in C++ is the same for classes and for structs.

```
__value struct SuperType
{
private:
  int m_int;

public:
  SuperType(int value)
  {
    m_int = value;
  }

  void Super()
  {
    Console::WriteLine("super type is {0}", __box(m_int));
  }
};
```

As with C++, managed value type variables directly contain their data. They don't simply point to their data.

Note the use of the **__box** keyword in the previous code. **__box** is used to box value types exactly as assigning the value type to **System.Object** works in C#. Because the previous **Write Line( )** function takes a garbage-collected class as a second parameter, you need to box the integer that's passed.

One problem with the garbage-collection algorithm is it moves objects in memory. This isn't a problem for managed code because the garbage collector automatically updates any references to the moved objects. However, this won't work when direct memory manipulation is required. To overcome this, the **__pin** keyword is used. This freezes the objects to a particular location in memory. The following code demonstrates how to use the **__pin** keyword.

```
CCurrentUser __pin* me = new CCurrentUser();
```

Notice the keyword applies to (appears before) the pointer, not to the data type or the variable.

The following table (Table 6-1) contains a list of some of the other C++ managed extensions.

Managed Extension Keyword	Description	C# Equivalent
__abstract	Decorates a managed class to prevent the class from being instantiated directly. Only the children of an abstract class can be instantiated, assuming they aren't also decorated with __abstract.	abstract
__box	Boxes value types, so they can be based as garbage-collected classes.	int i; object o = i;
__delegate	Declares a delegate. To declare a multicast delegate, use __delegate(multicast).	delegate
__event	Declares an event.	event
__gc	Decorates a class declaration to make a managed class.	class
__interface	Declares an interface.	interface
__nogc	Declares a class as unmanaged. Used when **#pragma** managed is specified.	N/A: All classes in C# are managed.

Table 6-1   *C++ Managed Extension Keywords*

Managed Extension Keyword	Description	C# Equivalent
__pin	Freezes an object to a particular location in memory, so the garbage collector won't move it. This enables you to save references to objects in unmanaged code.	fixed
__property	Declares a property within a managed class.	property
__sealed	Creates a managed class that cannot be derived from. Use in conjunction with **__gc** and **__value** keywords.	sealed
__try_cast	Used to wrap a cast so, if the cast fails, a **System::InvalidCastException** is thrown.	Automatically supported
__value	Declares a class or structure as a value type.	struct SuperType { ... }
__finally	Adds the C# finally syntax to a try catch block. Code within the finally block executes regardless of whether an exception is thrown. It provides a convenient mechanism for resource cleanup.	finally

Table 6-1   *C++ Managed Extension Keywords* (continued)

Note the addition of the **__try_cast** and **__finally** keywords. These add some additional functionality to the C++ language that isn't natively supported.

```
try
{
  WebRequest* myRequest =
    WebRequestFactory::Create(URL);

  stream = myRequest->GetResponse()->GetResponseStream();

  while((bytes_read = stream->Read(buffer, 0, max_to_read)))
  {
    total_bytes_read+=bytes_read;
    Console::WriteLine(Text::Encoding::ASCII->GetString(buffer));
  }
  return;
}
catch(Exception* e)
```

```
{
    Console::WriteLine(e->Message);
}
__finally
{
    Console::WriteLine(S"\n\n\nFinished dumping page!");
}
```

The previous listing is a sample showing how to use the **__finally** keyword. Developers must be aware of several caveats when they use Managed C++.

First, if you included MFC into your project, you need to write some special code whenever you use the **new** operator on a managed class. The reason for this is that MFC redefines the **new** operator in debug builds in order to track memory usage. Unfortunately, this redefinition is incompatible with the managed classes and the result is an error C3828, "placement arguments not allowed while creating instances of managed classes". To avoid this problem, you need to undefine the MFC macro for **new** each time you call **new** on a managed class. After instantiating the managed class, you redefine the macro. The following is some sample code that demonstrates how to do this:

```
System::String* message;
#pragma push_macro("new")
#undef new
  message =
    new System::String("Truly, you have a dizzying intellect.");
#pragma pop_macro("new")

System::Console::WriteLine(message);
```

The other caveats relate to intermixing your managed and unmanaged C++ code. First, you cannot inherit one type of class from the other. In other words, an unmanaged class cannot derive from a managed class and vice versa. This includes any template-based classes. In fact, you cannot use **__gc** or **__value** on template-based classes.

```
// error C3151: '__gc' cannot be applied to a template
template<class T>
__gc class CDerrived : public T
{
};
```

The previous code is invalid, therefore. To leave off the __**gc**, however, makes the derived class, CDerrived, unmanaged and, therefore, breaks the aforementioned rule regarding mixing and matching unmanaged types.

```
// error C2516: 'T' : is not a legal base class
// see reference to class template instantiation 'CDerrived
// <T>' being compiled with T=CCurrentUser __gc *
template<class T>
class CDerrived : public T
{
};
...
  CDerrived<CCurrentUser*> pcu;
```

Finally, you cannot declare managed types as a global or a static. The resulting error is "error C3145: '**g_user**': cannot declare a global or static managed object or a __**gc** pointer." In fact, you cannot even contain a managed object within an unmanaged class, as is done in the following code.

```
class CUnmanagedClass
{
    CCurrentUser* cu;
};
```

Aside from these caveats, using Managed C++ is a powerful environment to work in because it's so quick and easy to begin capitalizing on the wealth of functionality built within the .NET Framework directly from your *existing* C++ applications. Rather than porting any code to .NET, you simply change the compile option on the C++ compiler and, immediately, you can begin using the rich .NET framework. This can be done whether your C++ program was originally written using ATL, MFC, or STL. All these libraries interoperate "relatively" cleanly with the .NET framework classes. Managed C++ can serve as a substitute for both the CCW and the RCW because it can switch so easily between the managed and unmanaged world. Managed C++ can provide a means for writing custom CCW and RCW code. If you need to call COM components, you can directly call the various COM API, such as **CoCreateInstance( )**, just as easily as you could call any of the other Win32 API. Also, as with Visual C++ previously, no need exists to declare each API you'll call because this has already been done for you in the various C++ header files.

Migrating Code

In this chapter, we discussed various approaches for integrating legacy code into the .NET Framework. The interoperability support in .NET is pretty complete, fairly easy to use, and can be completely customized when needed. This support is also crucial to migration strategies because it allows an evolutionary (a step at a time), rather than a revolutionary (everything at once) approach. Through interoperation, legacy code can be transformed to .NET at a pace that makes sense. Sooner or later, if the integrated legacy code has any life beyond basic maintenance, it can make its way natively into the .NET platform.

Currently, two approaches exist for "automatic migration" from existing code to .NET. As we previously mentioned, Visual Studio.NET includes a utility that automatically upgrades a VB6 project to a VB.NET project. This transforms the project, but not the developer. To take advantage of the .NET features requires rewriting at least some portions of the application. While .NET makes a revolutionary jump because all code can be converted at once, it's really more of an evolutionary strategy in which the code can be rather quickly deployed on .NET, and then, over time, portions of the application, both new and existing, can be designed with .NET in mind.

Microsoft is also providing JUMP to .NET, which provides several tools to integrate existing Java programs into .NET. JUMP includes a utility that converts Visual J++ projects to C# projects. Here, the translation may be a bit closer to what is ultimately desired because the languages have so much in common. Again, this is a reasonable revolutionary strategy because, in theory, minimal work is required to get the Java code converted and running on .NET.

One of the trickiest issues in software development is adding useful functions to software, while maintaining compatibility with existing versions. Yet, as significant new technology is introduced, if it isn't quickly integrated into the product, the product finds itself left behind. .NET is certainly significant new technology that's already influencing software development and will continue to do so for years to come.

Once you start developing in .NET, there are several reasons beyond the basic "it's cool and new" type reasons for migrating all your code. This includes basic programmer efficiency, code consistency, ease of maintenance, as well as adding new capabilities that can provide significant features and functions to the delivered software program or Web service.

As a component software platform, .NET allows for and supports migration component-by-component or function-by-function. Exactly how this is done will, of course, be application-specific. Some critical questions to ask yourself when developing the migration plan include: What new features are the most important to your users? and, What are the critical support issues you're facing with your current applications? Answering these questions is the first step in developing a migration plan. The features at the top of the list dictate where .NET development starts and, hence, where the migration path begins. Over time, as new development is done, additional components can be brought on to the platform.

Summary

We've quickly come to the end of our discussions on C# and .NET. This book set out to give you a head start on C# and the .NET Framework. A short book such as this cannot go into the technical detail required in building a significant system, but, we hope it has given you an idea of what C# is all about, as well as some of the related topics that could be significant to your development. At a minimum, we hope we inspired you to install the .NET SDK (if you haven't already) and to get started programming in C#.

In addition to this book, several good resources are available for gaining further knowledge on .NET in advance of its official release. This includes the Microsoft Developer's Network site, which has a specific home page for .NET at http://msdn.microsoft.com/net/. A wide variety of other useful Web resources also exist.

Index

A

__abstract keyword, Managed C++, *206*
abstraction
    See also object-oriented features of C#
    interfaces and, 31–34
ActiveX components, COM (Component
    Object Model) and, 5
adapter classes, Java comparison, 137
AddRef( ) method, reference counting,
    152–153
ADO.NET classes, .NET Framework, 10
ApartmentState property, threading of RCW
    components, 176, 177
APIs, calling unmanaged from C#, 199–200
application domains, .NET Framework, 77–78
arrays, 27–28
    C++ comparison, 119–120
    Java comparison, 141
    multidimensional, 28
    overview, 27
    Visual Basic.NET comparison, 129
ASP.NET classes
    integrating legacy code with C#, 168, *169*
    .NET Framework, 9–10
assemblies, 76–77
    See also .NET Framework
    building, 78–79
    calling .NET objects from COM,
        177–178
    Java comparison, 134
    libraries, 77
    types of, 77
    version control, 79–84
assembly manifests, version control, 79–81
assignment and equality operators restriction,
    C++ comparison, 112–114
ATL programming, multiple inheritance,
    154–156
attribute-based programming, 86–88
    See also metadata; reflection
    PrimaryKeyAttribute, 87–88
attributes, 61–62
    COM interoperability, 193–194
    custom, 62
automatic generation of documentation, Java
    comparison, 133

B

binding
    early. *See* early binding
    late. *See* late binding
bool type, C# value types, *19*
__box keyword, Managed C++, 206
boxing and unboxing, type management, 25–26
ByeBye.cpp, Managed C++, 202
byte type, C# value types, *19*

C

C#
    attributes, 61–62
    calling COM objects from, 169–177

calling unmanaged APIs from, 199–200
coding style, 68
defined, 13–14
documenting code via XML tags, 66–67
exceptions, 59–61
highlights of, 14
indexers, 62–65
integrating legacy code with, 167–211
Java and, 13, 132–141
language comparisons, 109–141
limitations of, 143–166
namespaces, 57–59
.NET Framework, 2–11, 69–108
object-oriented component development,
     28–57
object-oriented features of, 29–39
overview, 1–14
pronunciation of, 2
reasons for using, 11–13
SimpleProgram example, 16–18
type management, 18–28
unsafe keyword, 65–66
value types, 19–20
C++ comparison, 110–127
     See also language comparisons; Managed
        C++
     arrays, 119–120
     assignment and equality operators
        restriction, 112–114
     building component libraries, 124–125
     calling libraries, 124
     ConditionalAttribute, 121–122
     converting types, 117
     data types, 116–118
     declarative order as insignificant, 112
     exception processing, 115
     explicit jump statements, 114–115
     foreach( ) statements and iteration,
        115–116
     memory management, 125–126
     multiple inheritance, 123–124
     native data types, 116–118
     NULL as keyword, 118
     overview, 110–111
     performance, 126–127

pointers (lack of), 118–119
preprocessors (lack of), 120–122
strings, 116–117
templates (lack of), 122–123
types, 116–118
versions, 111
void** pointer, 119
calling COM objects from C#, 169–177
     See also integrating legacy code with C#
     COM connection points, 174–176
     COM object lifetime and deterministic
        finalization, 174
     inheritance and RCW objects, 174
     method return values and HRESULTS,
        173
     overview, 169–170
     RCW (Runtime Callable Wrapper),
        172–173
     RCW objects and inheritance, 174
     SampleSrv.idl, 170
     threading of RCW components, 176–177
     TLBIMP utility, 171–172
calling libraries, C++ comparison, 124
calling .NET objects from COM, 177–195
     See also integrating legacy code with C#
     assemblies, 177–178
     CCW (COM Callable Wrapper), 177,
        185–187
     COM interoperability attributes, 193–194
     .NET events and COM clients, 187–193
     .NET to type library conversions,
        194–195
     overview, 177–178
     REGASM utility, 184–185
     threading of .NET components, 193
     TLBEXP utility, 178–183
calling unmanaged APIs from C#, PInvoke
     (Platform Invocation), 199–200
CCW (COM Callable Wrapper), 177, 185–187
     See also calling .NET objects from COM
     garbage collection, 185–186
     interfaces, 185–187
     IPatient interface, 186–187
     PatientMonitor class, 186–187
char type, C# value types, *19*

CheckReferenceCount( ) method, reference counting, 152
class constructors, 40–42
  See also object-oriented component development
  defaults, 41–42
  instance, 40–41
  static, 40–41
class definition and usage, Java comparison, 134–136
class destructors, garbage collection and, 42
class libraries, .NET Framework, 9
class variables, Managed C++, 204
classes
  See also structs
  abstract, 31–34
  adding to SimpleProgram example, 17–18
ClassInterfaceAttribute, TLBEXP utility and calling .NET objects from COM, 181
cl.exe compiler with /CLR option, Managed C++, 201
clients, defined, 50
CLR (Common Language Runtime)
  garbage collection, 42, 98–106
  loading, 72–75
  metadata and, 85–86
  .NET Framework, 6–7, 72–75
  version control, 81–82
CLS (Common Language Specification), .NET Framework, 8–9, 94–95
code, migrating, 210–211
coding style, 68
CoInitializeEx( ) call, threading of RCW components, 176
COM (Component Object Model), 4–5
  ActiveX components, 5
  callable wrapper. *See* CCW
  calling COM objects from C#, 169–177
  calling .NET objects from, 177–195
  components, 4
  connection points, 174–176
  containers, 5
  integrating legacy code with C#, 168–169
  interoperability attributes, 193–194
  .NET events and COM clients, 187–193
  object lifetime and deterministic finalization, 174
  OLE/COM Viewer and exporting IDLs, 179–183, 189–191
  servers, 4
COM connection points, 174–176
  See also calling COM objects from C#
  Countdown object, 174–175
  CountdownClient.cs, 175–176
  TimersAsm.Dll, 175–176
COM interoperability attributes, 193–194
  ComVisibleAttribute( ), 194
  GuidAttribute( ), 193–194
  overview, 193
  ProgIdAttribute, 194
Common Language Runtime. *See* CLR
Common Language Specification. *See* CLS
component libraries, C++ comparison, 124–125
component-based software development, 2–6
  See also .NET Framework
  COM (Component Object Model), 4–5
  monolithic approach versus, 3
  .NET Framework, 5–6
  object-oriented. *See* object-oriented component development
  OLE (Object Linking and Embedding), 2–3
  phases, 2–3
components
  ActiveX, 5
  COM (Component Object Model), 4
  threading of .NET, 193
  threading of RCW, 176–177
ComponentServices class, .NET Framework, 10
ComVisibleAttribute( ), COM interoperability attributes, 194
ConditionalAttribute, C++ comparison, 121–122
configuration files, version control, 82–83
connection points, COM, 174–176

constructors
  class, 40–42
  instance, 40–41
  static, 40–41
containers, COM (Component Object Model), 5
containment, 156–159
  See also limitations of C#; multiple
    inheritance
  defined, 158
  FileStreamRefCounted class, 157–158
  IRefCountedImpl class, 156–157
  substitutability and, 159
converting types
  C++ comparison, 117
  .NET to type library, 194–195
Countdown object, COM connection points,
  174–175
CountdownClient.cs, COM connection points,
  175–176
cross-language interoperability, .NET
  Framework, 93–94
cross-platform compatibility, Java comparison,
  133
CTS (Common Type System), .
  NET Framework, 95

D

data marshalling, 196–199
  See also integrating legacy code with C#
  EmployeeFactory class, 197–199
  isomorphic types, 196
  nonisomorphic types, 196
  overview, 196
  parameters, 196
  process of, 197–199
  strings and MarshalAsAttribute( ),
    196–197, 198
decimal type, C# value types, *19*
declarative order as insignificant, C++
  comparison, 112
declaring delegates, 51–52
declaring namespaces, 58–59
declaring variables, **using** keyword, 147–150
__delegate keyword, Managed C++, *206*

delegates, 50–53
  See also object-oriented component
    development
  declaring, 51–52
  instances, 51
  Java comparison, 138
  methods, 51
  multicast, 53
  type declaration, 51
delegation and events
  Java comparison, 136–138
  .NET Framework, 98
deployment enhancements, .NET Framework,
  7–8
destructors
  class, 42
  deterministic finalization and, 146
  garbage collection and, 104–105
  Managed C++, 203
deterministic finalization, 144–154
  See also limitations of C#
  COM object lifetime, 174
  destructors, 146
  Enter( ) calls, 146–147
  Exit( ) calls, 146–147
  explicit release of resources, 146–147
  Finalize( ) methods, 146
  .NET Framework, 153–154
  overview, 144–146
  reference counting, 150–153
  resource versus memory cleanup, 146
  try-catch-finally blocks, 147
  using keyword, 147–150
Dispose function, garbage collection, 105
Dispose( ) method, **using** keyword, 148–150
documentation, automatic generation of, 133
documenting code via XML tags, 66–67
domains, application, 77–78
double type, C# value types, *19*

E

early binding, TLBEXP utility and calling
  .NET objects from COM, 181
EmployeeFactory class, data marshalling,
  197–199

encapsulation, 39
> *See also* object-oriented features of C#

End With blocks, Visual Basic.NET
comparison, 131

Enter( ) calls, deterministic finalization,
146–147

Enum type conversion, .NET to type library
conversions, 195

enumerations, 22–23
> *See also* type management; value types
> Java comparison, 138–139

equality and assignment operators restriction,
C++ comparison, 112–114

error trapping. *See* exceptions

__event keyword, Managed C++, *206*

events, 53–57
> *See also* object-oriented component
> development
> IDispatch-based, 192–193
> .NET events and COM clients, 187–193

events and delegation
> Java comparison, 136–138
> .NET Framework, 98

exceptions, 59–61
> C++ comparison, 115
> Java comparison, 140

Exit( ) calls, deterministic finalization, 146–147

explicit conversions, type management, 26

explicit jump statements, C++ comparison,
114–115

explicit release of resources, 146–147

exporting IDLs
> *See also* .NET events and COM clients;
> TLBEXP utility
> OLE/COM Viewer, 179–183, 189–191

extending base class, inheritance, 30

extension keywords, Managed C++, *206–207*

extensions, Managed C++, 204–205

F

fields, object-oriented component
development, 46

FileStreamRefCounted class
containment, 157–158
interface implementation, 160–161

FileStreamRefCounted constructors,
reference counting, 152

finalization
> deterministic. *See* deterministic
> finalization
> garbage collection and, 102–105

Finalize( ) methods, deterministic finalization,
146

__finally keyword, Managed C++, *207*, 208

float type, C# value types, *19*

foreach( ) statements
> C++ comparison, 115–116
> Java comparison, 141

forms, .NET Framework WinForms, 9

freachable queue, garbage collection, 104

G

garbage collection, 98–106
> *See also* .NET Framework
> CCW (COM Callable Wrapper), 185–186
> class destructors and, 42
> destructors and, 104–105
> Dispose function, 105
> finalization, 102–105
> freachable queue, 104
> Managed C++, 202–203, 206
> managed heap, 99, 101–102
> overview, 98–99
> root objects, 100–101
> steps to, 100–102
> strong and weak references, 105–106

__gc keyword, Managed C++, *206*, 208–209

GetPKValue( ) function, reflection, 90–93

GetPrimaryKeyName( ) function, reflection,
89–90

global types, Managed C++, 209

GuidAttribute( ), COM interoperability
attributes, 193–194

H

HRESULTS and method return values
calling COM objects from C#, 173
.NET to type library conversions,
194–195

I

IDispatch pointers, .NET events and COM
clients, 189

IDispatch-based events, .NET events and COM
clients, 192–193

IDLs, exporting via OLE/COM Viewer,
179–183, 189–191

IL. *See* MSIL (Microsoft intermediate
language)

IMonitorEvent, .NET events and COM clients,
192

implicit conversions, type management, 26

inclusion polymorphism, 34–37
See also operation polymorphism;
polymorphism

indexers, 62–65
Java comparison, 140

inheritance, 29–30
See also object-oriented features of C#
combining macros with interface,
162–164
extending base class, 30
Managed C++, 208
multiple. *See* multiple inheritance
RCW objects and calling COM objects
from C#, 174

initialization, threading of RCW components,
176

instance constructors, 40–41
See also class constructors

instances, delegate, 51

int type, C# value types, *19*

integrating legacy code with C#, 167–211
ASP.NET, 168, *169*
calling .NET objects from COM,
177–195
COM (Component Object Model),
168–169
data marshalling, 196–199
integration approaches, 168–169
Managed C++, 201–209
migrating code, 210–211
overview, 168

PInvoke (Platform Invocation), 199–200

interface implementation, 160–162
See also multiple inheritance
FileStreamRefCounted class, 160–161
IRefCounted interface, 160, 161–162

interface inheritance, combining macros with,
162–164

__interface keyword, Managed C++, *206*

interfaces
abstraction and, 31–34
calling unmanaged APIs from C#,
199–200
CCW (COM Callable Wrapper), 185–187
Java comparison, 141

Interlocked class
reference counting, 152
thread synchronization, 108

intermediate language (IL). *See* MSIL
(Microsoft intermediate language)

interoperability
cross-language, 93–94
Managed C++, 201–209

invoking platforms, PInvoke (Platform
Invocation), 199–200

IPatient interface
CCW (COM Callable Wrapper), 186–187
.NET events and COM clients, 187–189

IRefCounted interface
interface implementation, 160, 161–162
reference counting, 152

IRefCountedImpl class, containment,
156–157

isomorphic types, data marshalling, 196

iteration and foreach( ) statements, C++
comparison, 115–116

J

Java comparison, 13, 132–141
See also language comparisons
adapter classes, 137
arrays, 141
assemblies, 134
automatic generation of documentation,
133

class definition and usage, 134–136
cross-platform compatibility, 133
delegates and events, 136–138
enumerations, 138–139
exceptions, 140
foreach( ) statements, 141
indexers, 140
interfaces, 141
JIT compilers, 132
metadata, 133
namespaces, 133–134
overview, 132–133
packages, 133–134
passing parameters by reference, 138
primitive types, 134
properties, 138
source files, 134
switch statements, 141
unsafe mode, 140
versioning, 133–134
JIT compilers
    Java comparison, 132
    metadata and, 86
jump statements, C++ comparison and explicit,
    114–115
JUMP tools, migrating code, 210

L

language comparisons, 109–141
    See also programming
    C++ comparison, 110–127
    Java comparison, 132–141
    overview, 110
    Visual Basic.NET comparison, 127–131
late binding
    TLBEXP utility and calling .NET objects
        from COM, 180
    Visual Basic.NET comparison, 127
libraries
    as assemblies type, 77
    C++ comparison and calling, 124
    C++ comparison and component,
        124–125
    generating COM-type via TLBEXP
        utility, 178–183

.NET Framework class, 9
.NET to type library conversions,
    194–195
limitations of C#, 143–166
    deterministic finalization, 144–154
    macros, 162–164
    multiple inheritance, 154–162
    overview, 144
    source code security, 166
    templates, 164–165
lock keyword, thread synchronization, 107
long type, C# value types, *19*

M

macros, 162–164
    See also limitations of C#
    combining with interface inheritance,
        162–164
    overview, 162
Main( ) declaration, SimpleProgram example,
    16–17
Managed C++, 201–209
    See also C++ comparison; integrating
        legacy code with C#; interoperability
    __abstract keyword, *206*
    adding code to native C++, 201–202
    __box keyword, 206
    ByeBye.cpp, 202
    caveats, 208–209
    class variables, 204
    cl.exe compiler with /CLR option, 201
    __delegate keyword, *206*
    destructors, 203
    __event keyword, *206*
    extension keywords, *206–207*
    extensions, 204–205
    __finally keyword, *207*, 208
    garbage collection, 202–203, 206
    __gc keyword, *206*, 208–209
    global types, 209
    idiosyncrasies, 208–209
    inheritance, 208
    __interface keyword, *206*
    MFC and, 208
    __nogc keyword, *206*

overview, 201
__pin keyword, *207*
pointers, 204
__property keyword, *207*
references, 205
__sealed keyword, *207*
static types, 209
__try_cast keyword, *207*
type variables, 206
__value keyword, 205, *207*, 208–209
managed execution, .NET Framework, 7
managed heap, garbage collection, 99,
   101–102
MarshalAsAttribute( ), data marshalling and
   strings, 196–197, 198
marshalling. *See* data marshalling
memory management
   C++ comparison, 125–126
   garbage collection and, 42, 98–106
metadata, 6, 84–93
   See also MSIL (Microsoft intermediate
      language); .NET Framework
   attribute-based programming, 86–88
   CLR (Common Language Runtime) and,
      85–86
   Java comparison, 133
   JIT compiler and, 86
   overview, 84–86
   reflection, 88–93
   version control and assembly manifests,
      79–81
method parameters, 43–46
   output parameter value, 44–45
   passing via values, 43
   variable, 45–46
method return values and HRESULTS
   calling COM objects from C#, 173
   .NET to type library conversions,
      194–195
methods, 42–46
   See also object-oriented component
      development
   delegate, 51

overview, 42–43
   parameters, 43–46
MFC, Managed C++ and, 208
migrating code, 210–211
   See also integrating legacy code with C#
   JUMP tools, 210
modules, 76
   See also .NET Framework
   building, 78–79
monolithic approach, component-based
   software development versus, 3
MSIL (Microsoft intermediate language), 5–6,
   70–75
   See also .NET Framework
   loading CLR (Common Language
      Runtime), 72–75
   metadata, 6
   overview, 70–72
multicast delegates, 53
   See also delegates; object-oriented
      component development
multidimensional arrays, 28
   See also arrays
multiple inheritance, 30, 154–162
   See also inheritance; limitations of C#
   ATL programming, 154–156
   C++ comparison, 123–124
   containment, 156–159
   interface implementation, 160–162
   overview, 154–156

N

namespaces, 57–59
   declaring, 58–59
   Java comparison, 133–134
   System, 57–58
native data types, C++ comparison, 116–118
.NET components, threading of, 193
.NET events and COM clients, 187–193
   See also calling .NET objects from COM
   exporting IDLs, 189–191
   IDispatch pointers, 189
   IDispatch-based events, 192–193

IMonitorEvent, 192
IPatient interface, 187–189
overview, 187
PatientMonitor class, 190–192
.NET Framework, 2–11, 69–108
ADO.NET classes, 10
application domains, 77–78
ASP.NET classes, 9–10
assemblies, 76–77, 78–79
building blocks of, 76–78
building modules and assemblies, 78–79
calling COM objects from C#, 169–177
class libraries, 9
CLR (Common Language Runtime), 6–7,
72–75
CLS (Common Language Specification),
8–9, 94–95
coding style, 68
component-based software development,
2–6
ComponentServices class, 10
cross-language interoperability, 93–94
CTS (Common Type System), 95
defined, 2
delegation and events, 98
deployment enhancements, 7–8
deterministic finalization, 153–154
garbage collection, 98–106
managed execution, 7
metadata, 84–93
migrating code, 210–211
modules, 76, 78–79
MSIL (Microsoft intermediate language),
5–6, 70–75
object-oriented nature of, 96–98
overview, 6, 70
security, 8
thread synchronization, 107–108
tools, 10, *11*
type system, 7
version control, 79–84
Web services, 9–10
WinForms, 9
.NET objects, calling from COM, 177–195

.NET to type library conversions, 194–195
See also calling .NET objects from COM
duplicate type names, 195
Enum type conversion, 195
method return values and HRESULTS,
194–195
versions, 195
__nogc keyword, Managed C++, *206*
nonisomorphic types, data marshalling, 196
NULL as keyword, C++ comparison, 118

O

object-oriented component development,
28–57
See also component-based software
development
class constructors, 40–42
class destructors, 42
delegates, 50–53
events, 53–57
fields, 46
methods, 42–46
object-oriented features of C#, 29–39
operator overloading, 48–50
overview, 28–29
properties, 46–48
object-oriented features of C#, 29–39
abstraction, 31–34
encapsulation, 39
inheritance, 29–30
overview, 29
polymorphism, 34–39
System.Object, 29
object-oriented nature of .NET Framework,
96–98
See also .NET Framework
System.Object, 96–97
objects, root, 100–101
OLE (Object Linking and Embedding),
component-based software development,
2–3
OLE/COM Viewer, exporting IDLs, 179–183,
189–191

operation polymorphism
>*See also* inclusion polymorphism;
>>polymorphism
>overloading and, 37–39
operator overloading, 48–50
>*See also* object-oriented component
>>development
>Visual Basic.NET comparison, 128–129
output parameter value, method parameters,
44–45
overloading
>operation polymorphism and, 37–39
>operators, 48–50

P

packages, Java comparison, 133–134
parameters
>method, 43–46
>passing by reference and Java
>>comparison, 138
PatientMonitor class
>CCW (COM Callable Wrapper), 186–187
>.NET events and COM clients, 190–192
performance, C++ comparison, 126–127
__pin keyword, Managed C++, *207*
PInvoke (Platform Invocation)
>*See also* integrating legacy code with C#
>calling unmanaged APIs from C#,
>>199–200
pointers
>C++ comparison, 118–119
>Managed C++, 204
>Visual Basic.NET comparison and safe
>>mode, 129
polymorphism, 34–39
>*See also* object-oriented features of C#
>inclusion, 34–37
>operation, 37–39
preprocessors, C++ comparison, 120–122
PrimaryKeyAttribute
>attribute-based programming, 87–88
>reflection, 89–92
primitive types, Java comparison, 134

ProgIdAttribute, COM interoperability
>attributes, 194
programming
>*See also* language comparisons
>attribute-based, 86–88
properties
>Java comparison, 138
>object-oriented component development,
>>46–48
__property keyword, Managed C++, *207*

R

RCW (Runtime Callable Wrapper), 172–173
>*See also* calling COM objects from C#
>objects and inheritance, 174
>threading of components, 176–177
reference counting, 150–153
>*See also* deterministic finalization
>**AddRef( )** method, 152–153
>advantages/disadvantages, 153
>**CheckReferenceCount( )** method, 152
>code listing, 150–151
>**FileStreamRefCounted** constructors,
>>152
>**Interlocked** class, 152
>**IRefCounted** interface, 152
>**Release( )** method, 152–153
reference types, 18, 23–25
>*See also* type management; value types
>comparisons, 25
>overview, 23–24
>strings and, 24–25
references
>Java comparison and passing parameters
>>by, 138
>Managed C++, 205
>strong and weak, 105–106
reflection, 88–93
>*See also* attribute-based programming;
>>metadata
>GetPKValue( ) function, 90–93
>GetPrimaryKeyName( ) function, 89–90
>PrimaryKeyAttribute, 89–92

REGASM registration utility, 184–185
    See also calling .NET objects from COM
Release( ) method, reference counting,
   152–153
resource versus memory cleanup, deterministic
   finalization, 146
resources, explicit release of and deterministic
   finalization, 146–147
root objects, garbage collection and, 100–101
Runtime Callable Wrapper. *See* RCW

S

safe mode, pointers and Visual Basic.NET
   comparison, 129
SampleSrv.idl, calling COM objects from C#,
   170
sbyte type, C# value types, *19*
__sealed keyword, Managed C++, *207*
security
     .NET Framework, 8
     source code, 166
Select Case statements, Visual Basic.NET
   comparison, 129–131
servers
     COM (Component Object Model), 4
     defined, 50
short type, C# value types, *19*
side-by-side installations, version control,
   83–84
signature key files, version control, 83
SimpleProgram example, 16–18
     adding class to, 17–18
     Main( ) declaration, 16–17
software development
     See also language comparison;
       programming
     component-based, 2–6
source code security, limitations of C#, 166
source files, Java comparison, 134
static class constructors, 40–41
     See also class constructors
static types, Managed C++, 209

strings
     C++ comparison, 116–117
     MarshalAsAttribute( ) and data
       marshalling, 196–197, 198
     reference types and, 24–25
strong and weak references, garbage collection,
   105–106
structs, 20–22
     See also classes; type management; value
       types
substitutability, containment and, 159
switch statements
     Java comparison, 141
     Visual Basic.NET comparison, 129–131
synchronization, thread, 107–108
System namespace, 57–58
     See also namespaces
System.IDisposable interface, **using** keyword,
   148–150
System.Object
     object-oriented features of C#, 29
     object-oriented nature of .NET
       Framework, 96–97
     templates, 164–165

T

templates, 164–165
     See also limitations of C#
     C++ comparison, 122–123
     System.Object, 164–165
thread synchronization, 107–108
     See also .NET Framework
     Interlocked class, 108
     lock keyword, 107
     typeof(<class>), 107–108
threading of .NET components, calling .NET
   objects from COM, 193
threading of RCW components, 176–177
     See also calling COM objects from C#
     ApartmentState property, 176, 177
     CoInitializeEx( ) call, 176
     initialization, 176

TimersAsm.Dll, COM connection points, 175–176
TLBEXP utility, 178–183
    See also calling .NET objects from COM
    ClassInterfaceAttribute, 181
    early binding, 181
    exporting IDLs, 179–183
    late binding, 180
TLBIMP utility, calling COM objects from C#, 171–172
trapping errors. *See* exceptions
__try_cast keyword, Managed C++, *207*
try-catch-finally blocks, deterministic finalization, 147
type management, 18–28
    arrays, 27–28
    boxing and unboxing, 25–26
    CTS (Common Type System) and .NET Framework, 95
    duplicate names, 195
    explicit conversions, 26
    implicit conversions, 26
    .NET Framework, 7
    .NET to type library conversions, 194–195
    overview, 18
    primitive types and Java comparison, 134
    reference types, 18, 23–25
    type comparisons, 25
    type conversions, 26
    unboxing and boxing, 25–26
    value types, 18, 19–23
type variables, Managed C++, 206
typeof(<class>), thread synchronization, 107–108
types
    C++ comparison, 116–118
    data marshalling, 196–199
    declaring delegate, 51
    Java comparison and primitive, 134

U

uint type, C# value types, *19*
ulong type, C# value types, *19*

unboxing and boxing, type management, 25–26
unsafe keyword, 65–66
unsafe mode, Java comparison, 140
ushort type, C# value types, *19*
using keyword, 147–150
    See also deterministic finalization
    Dispose( ) method, 148–150
    overview, 147–148
    System.IDisposable interface, 148–150

V

__value keyword, Managed C++, 205, *207*, 208–209
value types, 18, 19–23
    See also reference types; type management
    built-in functionality, 19–20
    comparisons, 25
    enumerations, 22–23
    listed, 19
    overview, 19–20
    structs, 20–22
values, passing method parameters via, 43
variable declaration, **using** keyword, 147–150
variable method parameters, 45–46
    See also method parameters
version control, 79–84
    See also assemblies; .NET Framework
    assembly manifests, 79–81
    CLR (Common Language Runtime), 81–82
    configuration files, 82–83
    metadata and, 79–81
    side-by-side installations, 83–84
    signature key files, 83
versions
    C++ comparison, 111
    Java comparison, 133–134
    .NET to type library conversions, 195
Visual Basic.NET comparison, 127–131
    See also language comparisons
    arrays, 129
    End With blocks, 131
    late binding support, 127

operator overloading, 128–129
overview, 127
safe mode and pointers, 129
Select Case statements, 129–131
switch statements, 129–131
With blocks, 131
void** pointer, C++ comparison, 119

W

weak and strong references, garbage collection, 105–106
Web services, .NET Framework, 9–10

WinForms, .NET Framework, 9
With blocks, Visual Basic.NET comparison, 131
wrappers
    CCW (COM Callable Wrapper), 177, 185–187
    RCW (Runtime Callable Wrapper), 172–173

X

XML tags, documenting code via, 66–67

INTERNATIONAL CONTACT INFORMATION

AUSTRALIA
McGraw-Hill Book Company Australia Pty. Ltd.
TEL +61-2-9417-9899
FAX +61-2-9417-5687
http://www.mcgraw-hill.com.au
books-it_sydney@mcgraw-hill.com

CANADA
McGraw-Hill Ryerson Ltd.
TEL +905-430-5000
FAX +905-430-5020
http://www.mcgrawhill.ca

**GREECE, MIDDLE EAST,
NORTHERN AFRICA**
McGraw-Hill Hellas
TEL +30-1-656-0990-3-4
FAX +30-1-654-5525

MEXICO (Also serving Latin America)
McGraw-Hill Interamericana Editores S.A. de C.V.
TEL +525-117-1583
FAX +525-117-1589
http://www.mcgraw-hill.com.mx
fernando_castellanos@mcgraw-hill.com

SINGAPORE (Serving Asia)
McGraw-Hill Book Company
TEL +65-863-1580
FAX +65-862-3354
http://www.mcgraw-hill.com.sg
mghasia@mcgraw-hill.com

SOUTH AFRICA
McGraw-Hill South Africa
TEL +27-11-622-7512
FAX +27-11-622-9045
robyn_swanepoel@mcgraw-hill.com

**UNITED KINGDOM & EUROPE
(Excluding Southern Europe)**
McGraw-Hill Education Europe
TEL +44-1-628-502500
FAX +44-1-628-770224
http://www.mcgraw-hill.co.uk
computing_neurope@mcgraw-hill.com

ALL OTHER INQUIRIES Contact:
Osborne/McGraw-Hill
TEL +1-510-549-6600
FAX +1-510-883-7600
http://www.osborne.com
omg_international@mcgraw-hill.com